NATALIE PORTER'S Immaculate Confections

BOOK ONE:
SUGAR FLOWERS

HELLO...

It all started about eight years ago when, on a bit of a whim, I decided that I was going to make mine and Chris' wedding cake. Friends and family questioned whether or not that was wise given how busy and stressful wedding planing is anyway, without the added challenge of producing a six tier cake version of a castle from The Lord of the Rings....

I fell in love with the craft and began to create cakes professionally, quitting my nice stable job training as an accountant. Over the next few years it was sugar flowers that really caught me as they gave such a great opportunity to explore design and colour. Creating cakes and sugar flowers is an art form, with that in mind I will always sacrifice realism in the name of good design, playing with shapes and colours to produce something that is interesting and eye-catching, as well as delicious. I was always conscious that in running a cake business one needed to be able to create flowers and foliage that were practical, quick and commercially viable - thus in 2016 the Rapid Rose was born. My methods for making roses, peonies, fillers, berries and foliage are quick and achievable, mastering these and using colour effectively will allow you to create such a wide range of styles and designs. Never underestimate the power of a little practice and remember to enjoy the process!

Over the last few years I have had the absolute pleasure of teaching many wonderful people how to create cakes and sugar flowers - it brings me such joy to see my techniques and products in action, helping fellow cakers to turn their bakes into works of art. None of this would have been possible without the support of my students and customers: thank you all!

I really do hope that you enjoy this book, a small introduction into my world of sugary art, and that you find the contents both useful and inspirational. It goes without saying that I would absolutely love to see anything that you create, so please do feel free to track me down via social media, my website or at a cake show and share your creations.

I can't wait to see where this mad journey into the world of cake takes me next!

Until the next book, happy caking!

Natalie x

CONTENTS

Practice, practice, practice...
And if it's not perfect don't
sweat it - no one is perfect
first time and practice
really does make perfect!

THE BASICS

Knowing where to start is a challenge with any craft. This chapter aims to break down the terminology, tools and techniques you will need to make sugar flowers. No-one is perfect first time, so don't be put-off if it takes a few attempts to master any of the techniques in this book. The most important thing you can do is practice, practice, practice… and enjoy the process!

PASTES

1. SUGARPASTE

This is the softest of the sugarpastes and the one that you would roll out and use to cover an entire cake. It's also called 'fondant' or 'roll-out' icing.

3. FLOWERPASTE

This is the hardest of the sugarpastes and is used for... yep, you got it!... making flowers. Like modelling paste it has gums in it for stretch and will be formulated so that it dries quickly and really hard. It's also sometimes called 'petalpaste' or 'gumpaste'.

Good flowerpaste will be soft, stretchy and strong. Generally speaking those made with natural gums (Gum Tragacanth) will be of a better quality (and more expensive!) than those made with manmade substitutes. Try a few out to find one you like and don't be frightened to mix two different products together to find the right combination for you.

2. MODELLING PASTE

This sugarpaste will be somewhat stiffer than fondant and is designed for modelling. It includes gums that make it more malleable and not crack as it's shaped (and by gums I mean natural or manmade substances that are edible and make it stretchy, like chewing gum is stretchy).

I'm often asked if you can just add some gums, such as CMC, Tylo or Gum Tex, to fondant to make a flowerpaste. Whilst they will stiffen the fondant and give it a little more stretch, it's not the same thing and the result when used won't be the same - you'll end up struggling against the paste rather than being able to focus on making the flowers.

COLOURINGS

1. GELS OR PASTES

These are highly concentrated and can be used to colour flowerpaste. The gel/paste itself is always fairly thick and therefore will not change the consistency of your flowerpaste too much. They're used throughout the book to colour the flowerpaste and fondant.

2. PETAL DUSTS & POWDERS

Petal dusts are powdered colours, used dry and brushed onto finished pieces to add shading, depth and realism. These are what will make your sugar florals look amazing!

Petal dusts are my absolute most favourite thing, so they have their own entire section later on, page 40.

BASIC TOOLS

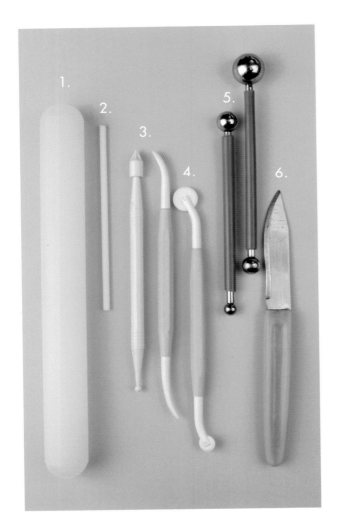

1. ROLLING PIN

For flower work you only need a small rolling pin. I like my pin to have a smooth rounded end as it can double-up perfectly as a giant ball tool.

2. TEENY ROLLING PIN

For extra fine work or thinning the paste having made a mexican hat, I use a plastic cake-pop stick... it makes the perfect miniature rolling pin!

3. MODELLING TOOLS

Purchasing a standard set of good quality modelling tools will be a good investment and great start to your collection of cake tools.

CONE / STAR TOOLS

These are used to make dimples or impressions of different shapes and sizes.

DRESDEN & VEINING TOOL

The pointed end can be used to make smooth lines and impressions. The other end, the 'little spoon', is excellent for poking and prodding things into place. This is my absolute favourite 'pokey tool'.

4. CUTTING WHEEL

Not essential, but a cutting wheel will make it easy to hand cut petals and leaves.

5. BALL TOOLS

I prefer metal ball tools as they've a better range of sizes, stick less often and due to their weight can be much more comfortable to hold and use.

6. KNIFE OR SCALPEL

I have always preferred to use a small paring knife as I find the slight curve to the cutting edge makes it easier to use.

7. WORK BOARD

A good quality, hard, non stick work board is perfect for rolling and cutting flowerpaste when making sugar flowers.

8. FIRM FOAM & MEXICAN HAT PAD

This is a foam pad used with a ball tool to stretch and shape your flowerpaste. A mexican hat pad is the same thing, but with holes cut in it for making filler flowers.

Pokey-Tool
[poh-kee tool] noun

Any tool or item with a pointed and pokey end that can be used to poke, prod or nudge flower paste petals, leaves etc. into place. Commonly used items include a range of sugarcraft modelling tools; less common are cocktail sticks, skewers, empty biros and tiny forks.

9. FLORAL TAPE

Available in a range of colours, floral tape is used to tape stamens to wires or tape elements together.

10. FLORAL TAPE CUTTER

This is a bonus item - a little block with razor blades inside that you can pull the floral tape through to cut it into narrower widths. You can of course do this by hand with scissors if you don't have one!

11. CUTTERS, PLIERS AND TWEEZERS

For cutting and bending wires when you arrange your flowers on the cake; long nosed pliers can reach into gaps and place flowers that are too small or fragile for your fingers. Tweezers are also used to add texture.

12. WIRES

Wires for floral work tend to come wrapped in paper to give them a colour - white or greens. Each wire has a 'gauge' number which describes thickness: low numbers for thick wires, high for thin.

13. HANGING RACK

This is just something that you can use to hang flowers or leaves on while they dry. For flowers made on toothpicks, I simply hang them with a peg.

14. DRYING FOAM

Shaped something like an egg box, it makes a great drying rack/former for sugar flowers and leaves.

15. CORNFLOUR

Cornflour is excellent at stopping things sticking, helping you to get a nice clean cut. You can also use it to prevent paste sticking inside moulds or veiners. Use sparingly as too much will dry your paste out. I like to use a pot and fluffy paint brush to dab a little corn flour where I need it as I find this the best way to control the amount I'm using, though you could also buy or make a 'puff' of cornflour.

16. POLYSTYRENE BLOCKS

An old cake dummy or other piece of polystyrene, is somewhere to put your flowers whilst working on them or whilst they're drying. When making peonies I push a drinking straw into my block so I can easily remove the flower without putting any pressure on the petals.

17. TREX OR PETALBASE

Trex is white vegetable fat, the same Crisco or Cookeen. Petalbase is a cake specific product that is basically the same thing, but with a little scent added. Use it to grease your fingers so that the flowerpaste doesn't stick. It can also be used to revive dry paste - see page 19.

18. ROYAL ICING

It dries rock solid and is great for attaching flowers to cakes and keeping them in place. I always keep a small piping bag of royal icing to hand, with just a very small tip cut into the end.

19. TEALIGHT

Yes, a little candle... trust me, all will become clear!

BASIC TOOLS - CONTINUED

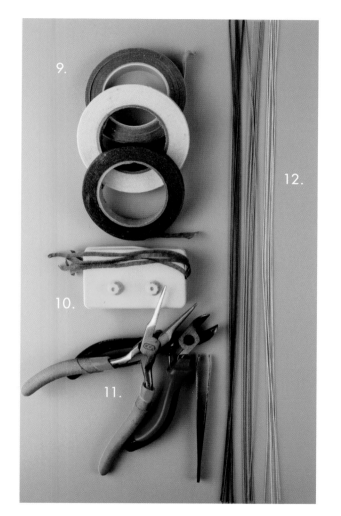

SPECIALIST TOOLS

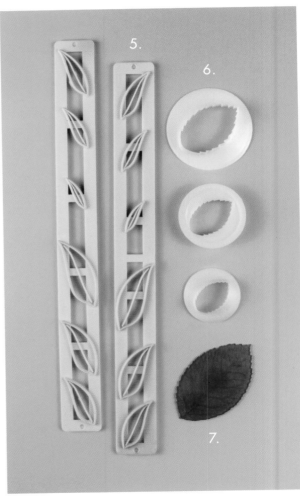

1. FIVE-PETAL ROSE CUTTERS

Available on my website in a range of sizes, my method taught in this book uses the same size for each row of petals, thus the size of the cutter dictates the size of the finished rose.

2. FIVE-PETAL PEONY CUTTERS

Just like the five-petal rose cutters, but with frilly edges for making peonies (also available on my website).

3. RAPID ROSE SUPPORT PAD

This is my baby... bright green, flower shaped and just a little bit squishy, it supports the petals whilst you work on the flowers. This is the tool that makes my method for both roses and peonies so very easy and therefore quick and practical.

4. VEINING STICK

When you roll the textured end of the stick over flowerpaste it leaves a pattern of veins. These are excellent multi-use tools, that can be used for a wide range of flowers. You can also use a wooden toothpick or skewer, rolling it over your flowerpaste in the same way but varying the pressure to create the ridges.

5. FOLIAGE ALLSORTS CUTTER

The FMM Foliage Allsorts Tappit makes excellent nad versatile branches when cut, wired and taped together.

6. ROSE LEAF CUTTERS

Commonly available in a set of three, the size variation is useful when designing sugar flower arrangements.

7. ROSE LEAF VEINER

Available in a variety of sizes, I'm a fan of the simple one-sided flat veining mat shown here (available within the FMM Veining Set, No. 1-4)

8. HYDRANGEA CUTTER AND MOULD

The best set for these and my absolute favourite is the Blossom Sugar Art Multi-set. The shapes are lovely and the mould is beautifully detailed.

9. CALYX CUTTERS

A calyx is the name give to the little green leafy bit that sits at the base of a flower. They're a perfect shape for making fabulous little fillers. A set of three small ones will be great as it gives you the option to make three sizes of flower.

10. POLY-BUDS

These form the centre of our roses and peonies. The size used depends upon the size of the flower you are making, so check out the end of the rose and peony chapters to see what sizes you're going to need. To make them, simply place a small dot of glue (from a low-melt hot glue gun) on the polystyrene ball and then insert the cocktail stick through it...

11. STAMENS

Available in a range of sizes and colours, stamens are little twists of paper with a blob on the end, used in the centre of flowers to add detail and realism. The filler flowers in this book use 'mini' stamens - the heads are at most 1mm in diameter.

12. POSY PICKS

Shaped like a small plastic test tube, these are used to attach wired flowers to a cake. Insert the posy pick into the cake, fill it with a little sausage of sugarpaste to support and hold the wires, and then place the wired flowers or leaves into the pick. Posy picks prevent the wires from posing a safety hazard by being directly inserted into the cake.

13. WATER BRUSH PEN

Use to stick things together, these are simply marvellous as you cannot accidentally spill it!

14. BRUSHES FOR DUSTING

I like to use make-up brushes as they're soft and available in a wide range of sizes. More on brushes on page 42.

If you don't have the exact same equipment as I do, use what you've got - as long as it's more-or-less the same the results will still be beautiful!

SPECIALIST TOOLS - CONTINUED

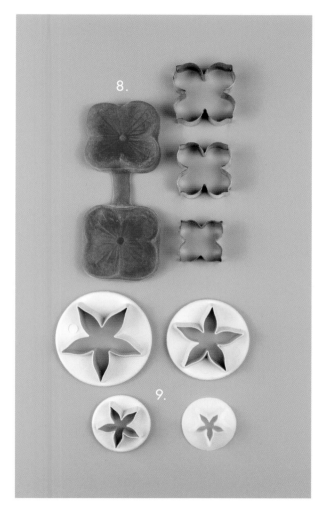

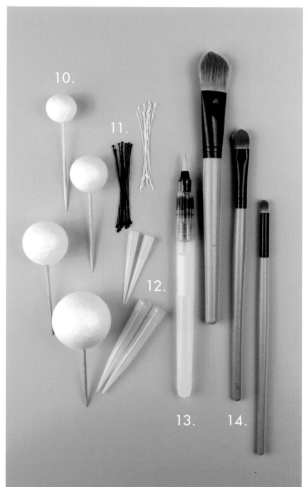

TECHNIQUES & TROUBLESHOOTING

It's no good having all this equipment if you don't know how to use it! These are the basic skills and techniques that we'll use throughout the book... and don't forget, practice makes perfect so if something doesn't go quite right the first time, smoosh it up and have another go!!

HOW TO COLOUR FLOWERPASTE

I will end up writing this a whole bunch of times so I may as well start here: go easy with adding colours as once it's in there you cannot take it away!! If you add too much and make a bolder colour than you were planning it will take a awful lot of white to bring it back and make it paler again... If this does happen, the best thing to do is take a fresh lump of white and add just a little bit of your too - dark flowerpaste to it at a time, that way you can control the colour and avoid making the same mistake again.

To illustrate how little colouring is required, here's 10g of flowerpaste coloured with SugarFlair Grape - you can see it doesn't take much to colour it or to make it slightly darker.

Go easy with colourings - you can always add more, but you cannot take it away again. Use pre-mixed sugarpaste for darker colours... so much easier!

KEEPING CONSISTENCY... CONSISTENT

When colouring flowerpaste the one thing we want to avoid is changing the consistency too much. To avoid this I tend to buy pre-made versions of very dark colours, in particular red, black and navy blue. Having bought them pre-made, I will then add in more colour or a different colour to tweak it to the shade I want, for example by adding Ruby or Burgundy gel colour to red paste, to make a deep and rich red.

TIPS FOR FLOWERPASTE

• Make sure you knead it really well and really warm and soften it up before use. The softer and warmer it is the easier it will be roll out thinly and the longer you will be able to work with it before it starts cracking or drying.

• Always keep flowerpaste you're not using covered up in cling film, a baggie or a pot. As it hardens so quickly it will start to dry if left out in the air and this will make it harder and eventually impossible to work with...
keep it covered!

• Each time you take some more paste from the pot or bag, knead it again so it's re-worked into itself and as soft/warm as when you started.

• If your paste does start to dry out, you can try adding in a little trex and/or water to bring it back. Do this with caution however as it can change and destroy the consistency of the paste. Sometimes you just need to abandon the lump of flowerpaste and start over with a fresh bit. Practice and experience will teach you when this is necessary or not!

• Should you find that the flowerpaste is sticking to you (likely to happen when you're adding colour), rub a little trex/petalbase on your hands and this should stop. It'll also keep your hands nice and soft! Use sparingly!

USE A PLASTIC WALLET

If you want to create a one-person production line, use a plastic wallet or a giant sandwich bag to keep cut shapes from drying out. Simply cut as many as you want, pop them in the plastic and they'll stay malleable and usable for quite some time... this is a great way to batch tasks and therefore work more efficiently.

ROLLING OUT

Make sure your flowerpaste is well kneaded.
Roll back and forth with an even and consistent pressure to
avoid creating lines or lumps in the icing. If your flowerpaste is sticking
to your board or rolling pin, use a very light dusting of cornflour to stop it.

THICKNESS: Leaves and flowers want to be fairly thin so that they look more floaty and realistic. Try to roll the flowerpaste out no thicker than around 1 - 2mm. The more you practice the easier this gets, so don't worry if your first few flowers look a little thick or clunky!

CUTTING WITH CUTTERS

Once your paste is rolled out, make sure it's not stuck to your work board - you can add a very light dusting of cornflour to the underneath of the paste if it is sticking. Place your cutter on the paste and press firmly all over... then give it a wiggle by moving the cutter side-to-side. This will help push the cutter through the paste and loosen it from the board (if the paste is sticking you won't be able to wiggle it). Pull away the excess paste from around the cutter. When you lift the cutter, if the paste comes with it you can run your palm over the cutter to push it further into the shape, thereby ensuring a really clean cut.

If you find that you're not getting a totally clean cut and that your shapes are a little rough or feathered around the edges, don't despair! Leave them be and they will very easily flick off once completely dry.

USING A BALL TOOL

This is a hard one to explain as it's all about pressure. If you're new to this, roll out some paste and experiment as that's the best way to learn precisely how much pressure will achieve what effect...Only use your ball tool when your paste is on the firm foam pad, using it on a totally hard surface will just squash and destroy the flowerpaste!

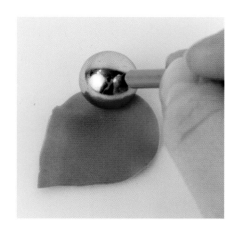

SOFTENING EDGES:

Hold the ball tool (or your rounded-end rolling pin) like a pencil. Imagine that you were tracing the outline of the shape - keeping the ball tool half on and half off your shape, sweep the ball tool back and forth to stretch and soften the edge. You're not trying to roll the ball tool, just hold it firm and sweep it along.

CUPPING AND EXPANDING:

Hold the ball tool in the centre of the leaf or petal and move it in even circles of increasing size. This will stretch the paste in all directions, making your overall shape a little thinner and a little bigger.

FRILLINESS:

The harder you press the more frilly you will make the edge of the flowerpaste. Frilliness is also affected by the size of the ball tool: generally speaking the smaller the ball the more frilly the result will be. This is why I like to use my rolling pin, especially for roses, as it's easy to get a nice even thinning and softness, rather than a frill!

WIRES

As wires are available in so many thicknesses, it's important to choose the right thickness and strength, for the job. Little leaves or berries only need a little wire, so a 28 gauge will be just fine. Bigger things, such as large leaves or fillers, would be better suited to a 24g or 26g gauge wire as they will be heavier and thus require a little more strength to support them. The really thick wires - 22g, 20g or 18g - are good for large, heavy flowers.

INSERTING WIRES:

This is another fiddly job which gets quicker with practice and experience. To make it easier I roll my flowerpaste a little thicker at one end so that I have a little extra thickness to insert the wire.

To insert the wire wet the end with a little water, hold the flowerpaste shape between your forefinger and thumb in one hand and with the other carefully insert the wire about 1/3 to 1/2 way up - your finger and thumb will be able to feel it inside the paste; you'll know if you've gone wrong!

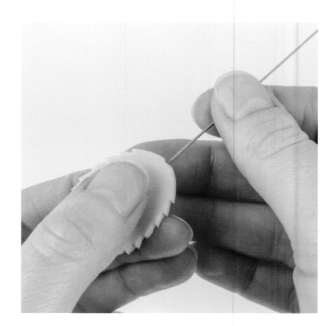

It's never a bad thing to have some spare leaves on hand so keep any that you practice on - they'll be useful on those occasions when you need just one more little leaf!

FLORAL TAPE

Most of the things we'll do with floral tape are super fiddly and thus do require a bit of practice to become quick and neat.

Floral tape is crinkled paper with a sort of gummy wax in the crinkles - make sure you stretch it out when you come to use it as this will expose the wax that will then stick to itself when warmed by your fingers.

Rolls of floral tape are usually 1/2" thick - wrapping that neatly around a teeny 28 gauge wire is almost impossible, so it's essential that you trim it down to a half, third or even quarter width. You can do this with a tape cutter or a pair of scissors.

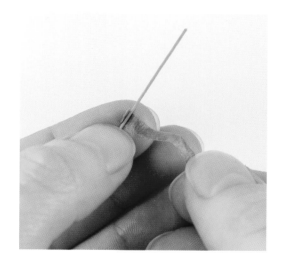

GETTING STARTED:

There are different ways to do this, but I find it easiest to place the tape and wire on my forefinger, pinch really tight with my thumb and then use my other hand to wrap the tape around the wire a couple of times. Once the tape is firmly attached you can spin the wire with one hand, using your other as a guide to hold and move it in the right direction. It's quick once you're used to doing it!

TAPING TOGETHER:

Using floral tape to tape things together is easy once you're used to using it. Simply attach the tape to your first wire and wind it round a couple times so it's firmly attached... then hold your second wire (leaf, filler, berry etc.) alongside the first and wrap the tape around both. With this basic technique we will be able to create bunches of berries, branches of leaves and more complex and complete floral units to place on a cake.

COLOUR

Colour is everywhere.

It's bright, dull, bold and lively... amazing, annoying, awe inspiring... it can make you feel sad and blue, or bring a smile to your face. Colour is everything.

For me, designing and decorating cakes is an art form. Baking does come into it, but the fun starts once that's all out of the way and you're sat in front of an iced and stacked cake - the perfect blank canvas.

Colour is super important in all aspects of art and design and it's no different when applied to cakes. Colour sets the tone for a design and will affect the way people react to it. A cool palette of white, silvers and iced blue would work a treat to conjure a feeling of winter, cold and snow. Spring and summer require warmth - all the pinks and lilacs with bright lively greens or sunflower yellows. Autumn is more reserved, lots of browns and rusty oranges, but still that small hint of life clinging on in bright yellows and rich reds. Do you see what I mean?

Understanding colour and how to use it will aid the design process, turning a fancy cake into a work of art!

THE COLOUR WHEEL

The first and most important step towards understanding colour is to know the colour wheel. There are two common versions of the colour wheel - knowing the difference between them and why it matters will help with your overall understanding of colours and how to use and mix them.

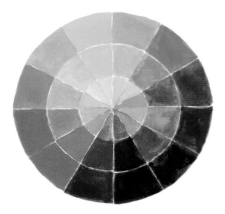

CYAN, YELLOW, MAGENTA

This colour wheel takes cyan, yellow and magenta as the primaries and as you can see this allows for so many more colours to be mixed! Yellow stays the same and you can still make 'primary' red and blue, but it allows for mixing truly bright pinks, purples, teals and everything in between.

Primary red is made from Magenta with a teeny bit of Yellow mixed in; primary Blue is made with Cyan and a touch of Magenta. There is no way to reverse-engineer the brightest pinks and blues using only red, blue and yellow. Think about your printer at home - the inks are described as CYMK: Cyan, Yellow, Magenta and K for black, almost as if the printer knows what it's doing and what it needs to mix all the colours!

This is the wheel I prefer and the one we're going to use in this book. There are two main areas of colour theory that we will look at: mixing colours and colour relationships. This lovely colour wheel will make a most excellent guide...

RED, BLUE, YELLOW

This is the traditional colour wheel that we've all seen before. It's hundreds of years old and is based around mixing three primary colours - red, blue and yellow - to make all the others. In principle it works but there is something missing...
Where are the bright fuchsia pinks or sky blues? Where is the Cyan and Magenta?! The RBY model does not allow us to mix some of the brightest most fun colours and so we are simply going to ignore it!

This wheel is dead to me...

HERE'S THE PROOF

Both these wheels have been painted on paper using watered-down food colourings. I did this to prove a point about mixing the colours and you can see that the CYM model is far superior! In reality there are so many shades and tones of food colouring available there is no need to mix everything from scratch, but it really helps to understand how it works!!

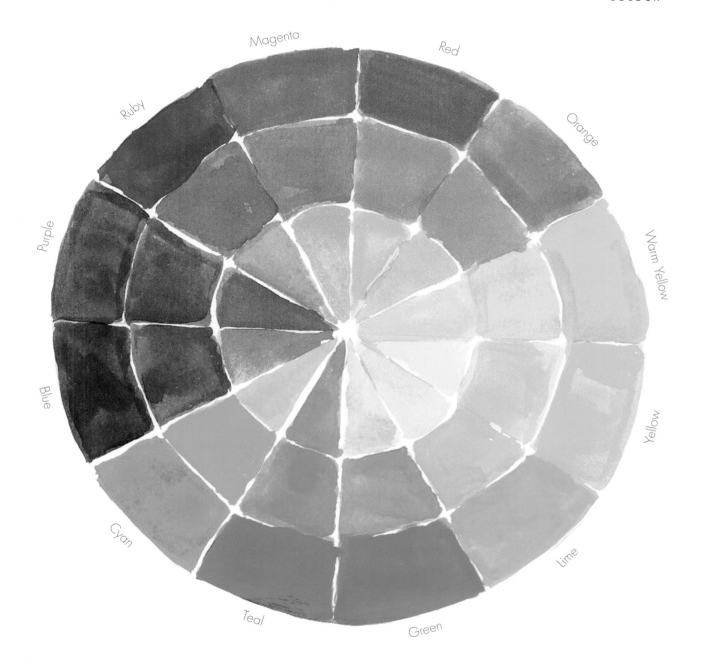

Magenta

Red

Ruby

Orange

Purple

Warm Yellow

Blue

Yellow

Cyan

Lime

Teal

Green

MIXING COLOURS

The main principle of colour theory is that by mixing the three primaries you can make all the other colours:

cyan + yellow = green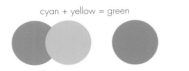

yellow + magenta = orange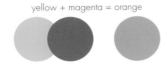

cyan + magenta = purple

By varying the amounts of each colour mixed together you can make hundreds of different colours - the colour wheel can help guide you in doing this... Say you want a deep rich plum. Look at the wheel and you can see that those deep purpleish colours are sat in between cyan and magenta, but closer to magenta - this tells you that plum will contain more magenta and reddish tones than blue. On the other hand, lavender is closer to cyan and must therefore contain more cyan and blues than magenta or reds.

Understanding how the wheel works and seeing that it shows you the 'recipe' for any colour will transform how you look at colour and enable you to mix pretty much any colour you like...

LIGHT AND DARK

If you start off with white icing, you can make a light/pale colour simply by adding only a tiny bit of food colouring. To make a darker version of the colour, just add more... don't forget that a little goes a long way so add the colour slowly and in small amounts. You can add a little black to make a really dark colour, but be wary! Black food colouring is made from combining high concentrations of all the other colours so it can dramatically change the colour you've mixed...

COLOURS FOR CAKES

Everything discussed above applies when colouring icing with food colours. As cake makers we're fortunate enough that there are dozens of brands making food dyes in hundreds of colours... so use them! There is no sense in mixing every last colour you use from scratch if you can take it straight from a pre-mixed pot, but it is good to know how to mix colours for those occasions when you don't have or can't find the exact one you want.

MIXING COLOURS: A STUDY IN GREEN

Take a look at the green part of the colour wheel.
On the one side of 'primary' green are all the shades
leaning towards yellow and on the other side all the
colours that head towards cyan and blue...

Hi! I'm Green...
I'm the favourite!

If we're aiming to make a lime green we need to add yellow as we can see that lime sits within the greens that are closer to yellow on the wheel... For a teal or turquoise, we need to add in some blue...

| RainbowDust: Leaf Green | + | RainbowDust: Yellow | = | Lime | | RainbowDust: Leaf Green | + | Wilton: Royal Blue | = | Teal |

And then by varying the amount of yellow or blue that we add, we can create a whole range of greens.
Don't forget you can also vary the amount of colour you add, making darker shades or a range of paler pastel shades:

The next thing to consider is the colours you are mixing or adding in - is it a primary blue or a sky blue? Primary yellow or a golden yellow? What shade of green have you started with?

All these things will affect how the colours mix and combine because they're not pure versions: Sky Blue is bright and vibrant leaning a little towards the tealy colours; Egg Yellow has an orangey tone to it; Navy is blue but a really deep and dark version... you get the idea!

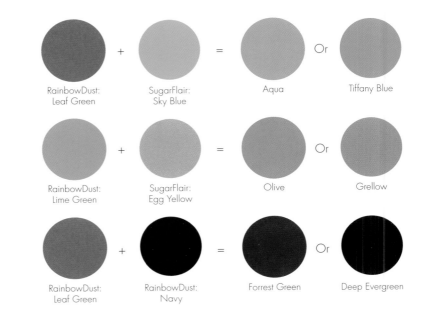

RainbowDust: Leaf Green + SugarFlair: Sky Blue = Aqua Or Tiffany Blue

RainbowDust: Lime Green + SugarFlair: Egg Yellow = Olive Or Grellow

RainbowDust: Leaf Green + RainbowDust: Navy = Forrest Green Or Deep Evergreen

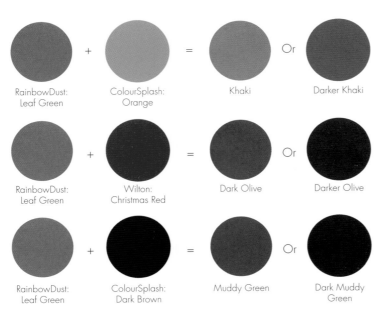

RainbowDust: Leaf Green + ColourSplash: Orange = Khaki Or Darker Khaki

RainbowDust: Leaf Green + Wilton: Christmas Red = Dark Olive Or Darker Olive

RainbowDust: Leaf Green + ColourSplash: Dark Brown = Muddy Green Or Dark Muddy Green

Having explored the green slice of the colour wheel, look at what happens if we add a little colour from the opposite side - reds, browns and oranges.

This is where we will find muddy and murky shades of green - these are some of the most interesting and realistic looking.

Use the reds sparingly as a little goes a very long way... too much and you'll have a made a mucky brown non-colour!

The final thing we'll look at with green is making vintage colours that are soft, delicate and feminine. As you can see, the addition of grey mutes the colour, making it soft and dull rather than bright or bold.

RainbowDust: Grey	+	RainbowDust: Leaf Green	=	Pale Sage	Or Sage
RainbowDust: Grey	+	RainbowDust: Lime Green	=	Vintage Olive	Or Vintage Lime
RainbowDust: Grey	+	RainbowDust: Eucalyptus	=	Pale Vintage Eucalyptus	Or Less Pale Vintage Eucalyptus

The best thing you can do to get good at mixing colours is to practice, practice, practice! Have a play, experiment and if you end up with a mid-brown sludgy colour, don't worry, bin it and start again!

A NOTE ON COLOUR NAMES:

The names given to colours are pretty arbitrary and almost always subjective. What one person thinks of as 'lavender mist' may be considered more of a 'lilac rain' by someone else... I find it best to pretty much ignore the name or description given for a colour and instead ask for a swatch to reference when I'm mixing and colour matching. Focus on the colour: How does it look? Will it work? Do I like it?

MIXING COLOURS: EVERYTHING ELSE

Here are some more of my favourite colours, often used for sugar flowers. As you look at and follow this guide, remember to think about the colour wheel and relate back to how the colours are made. Also remember that simply varying the strength of the colour - adding more white or starting with just a tiny bit of colour - can dramatically change how a colour looks and how it will interact with other colours.

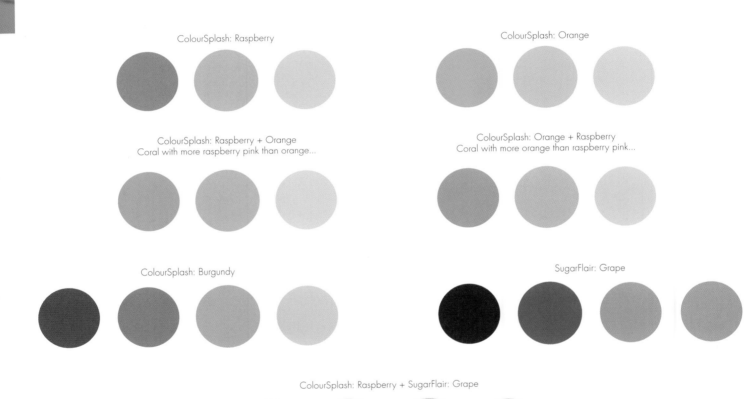

ColourSplash: Raspberry

ColourSplash: Orange

ColourSplash: Raspberry + Orange
Coral with more raspberry pink than orange...

ColourSplash: Orange + Raspberry
Coral with more orange than raspberry pink...

ColourSplash: Burgundy

SugarFlair: Grape

ColourSplash: Raspberry + SugarFlair: Grape

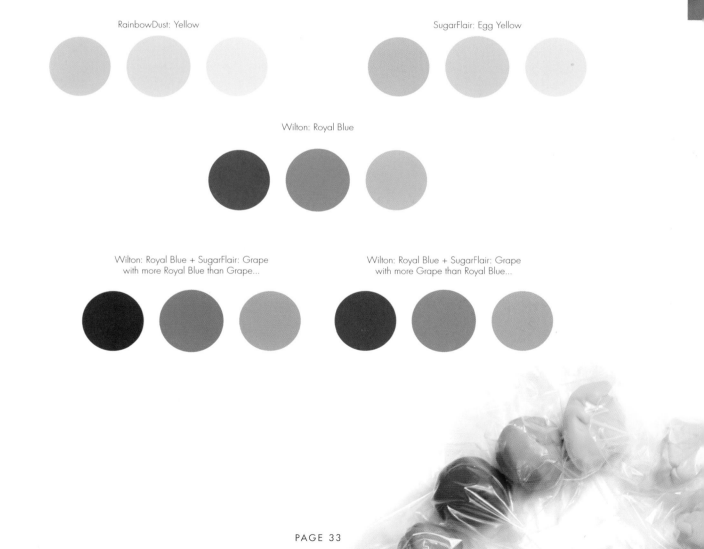

RainbowDust: Yellow

SugarFlair: Egg Yellow

Wilton: Royal Blue

Wilton: Royal Blue + SugarFlair: Grape
with more Royal Blue than Grape...

Wilton: Royal Blue + SugarFlair: Grape
with more Grape than Royal Blue...

COLOUR RELATIONSHIPS

The second area of colour theory that we're going to look at is colour relationships. This is just as important as being able to mix colours effectively - how you pair and match colours together to form a colour palette can make or break a piece of work. To keep it simple we'll focus on the two most important relationships: Contrast and Harmony.

CONTRAST

Contrasting colours will clash against one another and therefore they will appear to pop more brightly than colours that match. Contrasting colours are described as being 'complimentary' and can be found in pairs on the colour wheel - simply put, they're opposites:

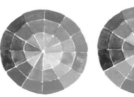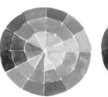

Reds & Greens

Blues & Oranges

Yellows & Purples

The fact that they clash somewhat is not always a bad thing when used carefully and with thought. We looked already at mixing variations of each colour: If we alter and tweak the shades and tones within our complimentary pairs we can begin to arrive at some very pleasing combinations that are rather more attractive...

Bright Pink & Lime Greens

Navy Blue & Sunny Orange

Purple & Shiny Gold

A NOTE ON RED AND GREEN:

The complimentary pairing of red and green never looks quite so harsh on the eye as the other two pairs do. This is for two simple reasons:

1. CHRISTMAS

The two main colours used to decorate for mid-winter festivities are green and red. This is largely due to nature as evergreen plants do just that - stay evergreen - and just about the only other colour you'll find in the landscape in winter is red (and sometimes a little orange) as the last few berries hang on through the cold.

 Ruby, Bright Red and Deep Green

2. NATURE

Lots and lots of plants have flowers which are within the pink and red family of colours. Almost all plants have green leaves and so pink/red and green is a combo that not only are we very used to seeing, but that nature itself has tried and tested over innumerable millennia...

It's also a combo that we see a lot on cakes, with pink being a popular choice of colour theme for weddings and events.

 Magenta, Pale Pink and Lime Green

Did you know the human eye can distinguish a greater range of reds and greens than of any other colour? We're programmed to like looking at this combination!

HARMONY

Harmonious colours are ones which match; they come from adjacent slices of the colour wheel and will always feel and look happy together... they don't clash or contrast, but rather blend and work together.

Floral work always looks best when a range of harmonious colours have been used in place of a single colour. Rarely in nature are things just one colour - even something as simple as a square inch of grass will contain a whole bunch of different greens as well as some browns, whites and yellows... So for example, instead of just pink and green, try using pink with a purpley pink, alongside a lime green and another green with a slightly darker tone - the finished piece will look so much more interesting!

This

looks way more
interesting than

this

You can also vary the intensity of a colour to achieve this natural
looking variation, by using a darker and paler shade of your main colour.

Also bear in mind the type and quantity of flowers and foliage you're going to use as you don't need to use each colour in equal measure.

A large rose for example, will be a pretty big chunk of colour, but a few berries here and there or a couple of filler flowers, not so much. Used wisely, a bright and contrasting bud or berry can really make the rest of your flowers and foliage sing!

A little pop of bright golden yellow and we have ourselves a choir!

The last thing to consider when putting a colour scheme together is the colour of the cake itself. This can have a huge impact on the overall feel of a piece - think about how much colours 'pop' on a black background, or how a floral arrangement might look on a cake iced in a contrasting or complimentary colour.

Bold Contrast

Soft Contrast

Harmonious

The colours of the flowers are on the harmonious side, being orange and a bright magenta, paired with khaki and limey greens. The navy base colour forms a complimentary pair with the orange giving high contrast and a very bright look.

The flowers on this cake are pale blue and peach, which actually make a complimentary pair. As they're so pale however it doesn't appear too bold... the background is a pale peach which looks much more interesting than plain white!

This design is one big exercise in using harmonious colours as they are all from the blue-purple-pink slice of the colour wheel. Drama and contrast are created through the use of light and dark shades, rather than by having a complimentary colour.

KEEP IT SIMPLE: MONOCHROME

This one can sound a little boring as it refers to either black and white or varying tones of just the one colour... but it's getting a special mention here as it gives us one of my most favourite colour combos: Green and White.

Beautiful, simple and elegant, with bright light greens it'll look fresh and new; with deeper greens it'll look more serious and mature... think of the first buds of spring or crisp white snow alongside evergreen trees!

Sometimes less is more and white and green is all you need!

A combination of monochrome and/or harmonious colours is what gives us the popular ombré trend that's been featured on everything from cake designs to hair dye in the last couple of years. Ombré designs can feature just the one colour, fading from dark to light or more than one colour fading smoothly into the next.

Depending upon the colours you choose it can look soft and pretty or bright and bold - it's a good way to add interest to a simple colour scheme and create something that's modern and contemporary looking.
Use the colour wheel to guide you as you mix the colours to create an ombré palette...

BE EXPERIMENTAL...

If you're not sure about a particular colour combo, test it!

You could do this with simple sketches and colouring pencils, with small swatches of icing or digitally on a computer. Put the colours together and see how they look, making substitutions until they work and look right.

I'm a big advocate for always sketching cake designs - you don't need to be a master artist and it will really help to give you a good idea of how the cake design will turn out. You can play with colours, shape, size, the placement of flowers...

From a commercial point of view it's useful too as you can give your customers a very good idea of what their cake will look like and make sure that all the details have been sorted out. When you then come to make the cake, all you have to do is make the picture and if it looks the same you can rest assured that you have done a good job!

Sketches are an essential part of the design process...

If you're struggling for a colour palette you can always pinch inspiration for colours from almost everywhere - nature, fashion, landscapes... even your favourite piece of wrapping paper! Have a quick search on the internet as there are a ton of websites which do this for you, providing ready-made images like this one.

PETAL DUSTS

This may sound like a bit of an exaggeration, but petal dusts really are my absolute most favourite thing and the BEST part of making sugar flowers. They give you a whole new dimension of depth and colour to play and experiment with, making sugar florals look bright, vibrant and realistic. I just love them!

In the previous pages we've looked at how to mix colours and create colour palettes that contrast or harmonise. Petal dusts give us another way to use and exploit these principles for awesome looking results.

The final colour of a finished flower will be a combination of the flowerpaste used to make it and the petal dusts brushed on top... you need to be thinking about the dusts you will use as you prepare and colour your flowerpaste.

VIBRANT

The colour you can achieve with petal dusts will always be more bright and vibrant than how flowerpaste will look alone... You can achieve a range of effects just by varying how much dust you add.

Raspberry
+ SugarFlair Plum

Grape
+ SugarFlair African Violet

Lime
+ EdAbleArt Kiwi

Khaki
+ Squires Leaf Green

HARMONY

You can add a dust in a colour(s) that harmonises with the colour of your flowerpaste, thus achieving subtle tones and gradients, with one colour fading into the next...

Raspberry
+ SugarFlair Plum
+ SugarFlair African Violet

Coral
+ RainbowDust Pale Terracotta
+ SugarFlair Plum

Pale Sage
+ RainbowDust Pale Pear
+ Fractal Olive Green

Lime
+ Squires Leaf Green
+ RainbowDust Claret

CONTRAST

Adding a little petal dust in a complimentary colour can do amazing things... this is especially useful for leaves, where adding a touch of something red, orange or brown to the edges of a leaf will create both depth and realism.

Olive
+ Fractal Fresh Green
+ EdableArt Tangerine

AN IMPORTANT NOTE ON FOOD SAFETY:

Each country has slightly different laws governing the use of colours in food. This means that some dusts are classed as 'craft dusts' and are thus not deemed to be edible. They are however non-toxic and therefore safe for food contact. In the UK these typically include many of the brightest pinks and purples, as well as some metallic dusts. You can use them on elements that will be removed from the cake prior to eating; fortunately sugar flowers are always removed and so it's OK to use non-toxic craft dusts. Be sure to check the type of products you're using and to use them appropriately.

BRUSHES

My favourite type of brushes to use for applying petal dusts are make-up brushes. They are readily available, nice and soft and come in a wide range of shapes and sizes. These are the three shapes/sizes I use most often:

WIDE SOFT BRUSH
The bristles are approx. 2cm wide and 3cm long, set flat in the ferrule. This one is perfect for the edges of roses and peonies, and for covering larger areas with lots of colour.

MEDIUM SOFT BRUSH
The bristles are approx. 1cm wide and 1.3cm long, set flat in the ferrule. It's good for smaller items that require a little more precision, such as the edges of leaves or filler flowers and berries.

SMALL POINTED BRUSH
The bristles are approx. 0.5cm wide and 1cm long, set as a cylinder in the ferrule rather than flat like the other two. These are great for detail and adding colour to the centre of fillers.

TECHNIQUES
I always tap or spoon my dusts out onto a piece of kitchen paper - I find the texture is a good surface to sort of 'hold on' to the dust while I'm mixing colours or loading my brush. It also makes a little less mess and doesn't risk staining your work board.

Cutting a drinking straw at an angle will make a most excellent tiny spoon!

Petal dusts are best applied slowly, with just a little loaded onto the brush. Take a little dust onto your brush and then rub it off onto the paper - the best way to describe why you must do this, is to say that you want the dust *in* the bristles rather than *on* the bristles. If you don't do this you risk picking up a large granule of colour and then smearing it onto your sugarwork, making a big, unwanted streak of colour.

You can always add more colour... but you can't take it away once it's on!

Use gentle, repetitive motions to apply the dust. It's better to repeat an action a dozen times than to go heavy handed the once and ruin your flower. The repetition will also serve to blend the colours onto the flowerpaste, creating a smooth gradient.

CLEANING:

If you want to clean a dusting brush, it's best not to use water and/or soap as this can damage the brush by 'setting' the colour. Instead, swish the brush around in a cup of cornflour and most of the colour will be removed, clinging instead onto the cornflour.

It's impossible to completely clean colour from your bushes, so it's best to build up a collection that allows different brushes for different ranges of colours - you'll never get enough purple out of a brush that you can use it with yellow, without tainting... A good excuse to have lots of brushes!

Each chapter includes instructions on how to dust each specific flower or leaf etc.

ROSES

Roses are romantic, beautiful and available in hundreds of different colours - you can always find a rose to suit your colour palette! They also come in a variety of sizes - big enough to use just a single bloom or small enough to use in clusters within a larger design. Being so versatile, they're an essential sugar flower to master.

ROSES - YOU WILL NEED:

- Basic Tools • 90mm five-petal rose cutter • Rapid Rose support pad
- 20mm poly-bud • Approx. 50g flowerpaste
- Colours used: ColourSplash Raspberry with SugarFlair Plum dust

This step-by-step makes a rose using a 20mm Poly-Bud and a 90mm cutter. Page 55 at the end of this chapter explains how to make other sizes.

1. Start with a Poly-Bud: a polystyrene ball hot-glued to a cocktail stick.

2. Make a cone of flowerpaste and using a little water, attach it to the poly-bud... squish it on to make the bud a little pixie hat! By making the polystyrene ball a little hat of flowerpaste, the ball becomes bud shaped *and* the tip of the bud is the same colour as your rose. There won't be any white peeking through that first petal...

3. Roll out some flowerpaste to a thickness of no more than 1mm. Cut a partial shape with the five-petal cutter and use a knife or cutting wheel to extract a single petal.

4. Place the petal on to your firm foam pad and use a ball tool (or the end of your rolling pin!) to thin the edges. You only want a soft wave, so don't make it too frilly.

5. Flip the petal over and place it so it's horizontal, tip to curve. Wet the bottom half of the petal.

The first petal goes on sideways. This is essential as it gives you more to wrap around the bud, making a perfect tight curl for the centre.

6. Place the petal on the poly-bud, so that the petal extends about 5 - 8mm above the poly-bud.

7. Fold the tip of the petal in first. To get a nice tight curl at the top you need to pull it in and down as you wrap it round. Use a little more water to hold it in place if needs be.

The sides and base of the bud and petal won't be visible in the finished rose, so don't worry if you tear or crack the flowerpaste.

8. Fold in the remaining side of the petal, again pulling it down a little to make a tight, cone shaped curl for the rose centre.

9. Roll out the flowerpaste and cut a full five petals with the five-petal cutter. Place it on to the firm foam pad and use the ball tool to soften the edges. As with the central petal, you're aiming for a soft wave so don't press too hard or make it too frilly.

10. Place the five-petal shape upside down on the Rapid Rose pad. Wet the centre and draw a line of water on the straight edges of each petal, up to where the curve starts.

11. Take your bud and insert it through the centre of the flowerpaste and through the hole in the Rapid Rose support pad. As you can see the pad supports the petals so they don't break or tear whilst you work to arrange them and form the rose!

The petals on a rose curl away from the centre. Using the ball tool makes the petals curl towards you, so by flipping them over before attaching them...

12. To make the first row of petals, attach one side of two opposing petals. As we're dealing with five petals, there isn't a true opposite, but as you can see they're tough enough to be pulled into place so they are more or less opposite one another.

... you take advantage of that curl and they will naturally want to fold away from the centre of the rose.

13. Pull the open side of the petals round and attach them so that they sit on top of the first side we stuck down, forming an interlocking over - under - over pattern. Pinch and adjust the petals, curling the edges back a little, so they look as if they are opening.

14. To make the second row of petals, attach one side of the three remaining petals. Try to place them so they are evenly spread out - you may need to pull them a little to one side or the other to do so but that's fine.

15. Pull round and attach the open sides of the petals, making the same interlocking pattern. Each petal sits under its neighbour on one side, then on top on the other...

16. Flip the rose over, remove the Rapid Rose pad and firmly press the petals onto the base of the bud. Use your thumb and forefinger to curl the top edges of the petals back a little. Try to make it look natural, as if the petals are gently unfurling...

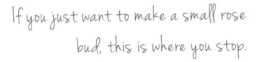

If you just want to make a small rose bud, this is where you stop.

17. Cut a second five-petal shape and once again use a ball tool to soften the edges and create a soft wave. Use the ball gently in the centre of each petal to make them a little bigger. Curl the top edges of each petal back a bit, accentuating the wave and curl made with the ball tool.

18. Flip the shape over onto the Rapid Rose pad and wet as before, in the centre and a line up the edge of each petal.

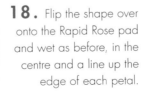

19. Insert the rose bud and choose a petal to start with, attach one side of it and then do the same for the next petal. Before moving on, attach the second side of the first petal, on top of the first side of the second petal. They should all overlap like fish scales, interlocking with that same over - under pattern that you made before with the previous rows of petals.

If your flowerpaste is very soft or conditions are damp and humid, wait a few minutes before flipping and attaching the petals so they can set up and dry a little...

Mind the Gap!

For a realistic rose, the gaps and spaces between the petals are as important as the petals themselves. Try not to squash everything too much so those gaps are preserved and realistic looking.

20. Continue overlapping and attaching the petals, going round until all five have been used. The final petal should overlap the first petal you attached, completing the interlocking pattern all the way around the rose.

21. Flip the rose over again, remove the Rapid Rose and press the petals firmly at the base so they're well attached.

Look at the top of the rose and adjust the shape and position of the petals so it looks open and natural - the strength comes from the bottom part, the top just needs to look pretty! Use a pokey tool to push the petals out a bit if you find they've become a little squashed.

This is your small rose - if you're only after little ones you can stop here.

22. Cut a third and final five-petal shape and an extra two single petals. Use a ball tool to soften the edges and make the petals a little bigger like before. Do the same to the extra petals and cut off the tip of the point. Curl the edges and leave to harden for a couple of minutes... then flip it on to the Rapid Rose pad and wet as before. Flip the single petals and wet up each side and across the bottom.

23. Attach the petals like the previous row, but this time pull them a bit closer together. Once you have attached three petals slot in an extra petal, maintaining the interlocking pattern...

24. Attach the remaining two petals from the five-petal shape - you should be left with a gap to insert the final extra petal. Flip the rose over and remove the Rapid Rose pad...

There are a lot of petals involved now so I would recommend drying the rose upside down for a bit to set... you can use a clothes peg to attach it to your drying rack.

25. Whilst upside down you'll be able to see if all the petals are equally spaced out and can shuffle them along if needs be. Check from the front that everything looks well placed and even, then press all the wet edges down firmly so everything is well attached and solid.

SOME OTHER HINTS AND TIPS:

• For a quicker finish you can save a little time by having an outer row of another five petals: one, two, three, five and *another* five. It looks almost the same and saves some valuable time...

• The Rapid Rose works best when you hold it firmly - grip the cocktail stick beneath the bud nice and tight so it doesn't move or wobble while you work.

• The size of the cutter dictates the size of the finished rose. Bear this in mind as you design and make them - sometimes a mix of sizes will work well together and other times it works best if you use one size, but mix up how finished the roses are. ie. buds, medium and full roses.

• Sometimes you'll end up with a feathery edge on your petals as a result of the cutter and ball tool. Fear not as these little bits will easily flick off once dry.

• If your paste is a bit floppy, for example because you've added a lot of colouring or the weather is really damp, you may want to let everything dry a bit between adding rows of petals.

• If you have lots of roses to make set up a conveyor belt: make all the buds and first petals, then do all your first five-petals, then the second rows and so on... You can cut a whole load of petals and keep them fresh in a plastic wallet, ready to use.

Have you ever met a bride who on her wedding day is going to count how many petals there are on her sugar roses?! ...No, me neither!

Unfortunately an error slipped through the editing and proofing process on Pg.55: where the book states you should use a 20mm poly-bud for the 100mm and 120mm rose cutters, it should in fact say to use a **25mm poly-ball**, as in the corrected chart below. Please keep this with the book for future reference.

I'm so sad and disappointed that I missed it and went to press with this mistake included, however I do hope that you are enjoying the book....

CORRECTED SIZE CHART FOR ROSES:

Each rose is made with only one size of cutter - the bigger or smaller the cutter, the bigger or smaller the finished rose will be. Therefore, the size of the cutter will dictate the size of Poly-Bud required and size of the finished rose. This table shows the sizes I recommend, approximate amount of flowerpaste required and roughly how big a full, finished rose will be:

60mm Cutter	70mm Cutter	80mm Cutter	90mm Cutter	100mm Cutter	120mm Cutter
+ 12mm Bud + 30g flowerpaste = 5cm Rose	+ 20mm Poly-Bud + 35g flowerpaste = 5.5cm Rose	+ 20mm Poly-Bud + 40g flowerpaste = 6cm Rose	+ 20mm Poly-Bud + 50g flowerpaste = 7cm Rose	+ 25mm Poly-Bud + 65g flowerpaste = 8cm Rose	+ 25mm Poly-Bud + 75g flowerpaste = 9.5cm Rose

This one is tiny and only needs a weeny bud - make it from flowerpaste, about 12mm diam. and dry overnight

DUSTING:

Use a wide soft brush to apply the petal dust. Keep your strokes light and always aim from the outside of the rose towards the centre - this makes it harder to go wrong and leave an unsightly blob of dust somewhere it doesn't belong. Build the layers of colour slowly, adding a little at a time.

Remember: you can always add more colour but you can't take it away again... go slow and easy with the petal dust, adding colour in layers until you achieve the depth of colour you're after.

SIZES:

Each rose is made with only one size of cutter - the bigger or smaller the cutter, the bigger or smaller the finished rose will be. Therefore, the size of the cutter will dictate the size of Poly-Bud required and size of the finished rose. This table shows the sizes I recommend, approximate amount of flowerpaste required and roughly how big a full, finished rose will be:

60mm Cutter	70mm Cutter	80mm Cutter	90mm Cutter	100mm Cutter	120mm Cutter
+ 12mm Bud + 30g flowerpaste = 5cm Rose	+ 20mm Poly-Bud + 35g flowerpaste = 5.5cm Rose	+ 20mm Poly-Bud + 40g flowerpaste = 6cm Rose	+ 20mm Poly-Bud + 50g flowerpaste = 7cm Rose	25 + 20mm Poly-Bud + 65g flowerpaste = 8cm Rose	25 + 20mm Poly-Bud + 75g flowerpaste = 9.5cm Rose

This one is tiny and only needs a weeny bud - make it from flowerpaste, about 12mm diam. and dry overnight

PEONIES

Peonies bloom from late-spring to early-summer and there is no other flower quite like them. With dozens of giant frilly petals they look like giant pom-poms and are a glorious sight to see! One often thinks of peonies as pink, but they also grow in white, yellow, peach and a deep rich pinky-red colour.

PEONY - YOU WILL NEED:

- Basic Tools • Rapid Rose support pad • Five-petal peony cutter, 120mm and 150mm
- Veining stick • 40mm poly-bud • Approx. 70g flowerpaste • Polystyrene block and drinking straw
- A couple bits of kitchen towel • Colours used: ColourSplash Raspberry with SugarFlair Plum and Squires Pink dusts

1. Roll the paste to around 1mm thickness. Use the 120mm cutter to cut out only part of the peony shape as shown...

This step-by-step makes a large peony using a 40mm bud and 120mm & 150mm cutters - see page 66 for info on other sizes and poly-buds.

2. Turn the cutter 180° and cut again, to make a roughly circular shape.

3. Press the edge of one of the petals onto the circle gently, to leave an impression of petals. Change the petal you're using and repeat, turning the circle so they don't overlap... you want it to look like the top of a peony bud, where the petals meet and have not yet opened.

4. Wet the top of the poly-bud and attach the circle, smoothing it down so it covers the top.

5. Roll out some flowerpaste and use the 120mm cutter to cut the first set of petals. Cut between each petal, making them more individual and giving more movement.

6. Place the petals onto the firm foam pad and use a medium sized ball tool to soften and thin the edges of the petals...

7. Place the petals back onto your hard work board and use the veining stick to add veins and detail to the petals: place the stick on the petals, with the tip in the centre. Keeping the tip in place, roll the rest of the stick back and forth in an arc, adding veins in a fan shape. Repeat for each petal.

8. Put the peony shape back onto the firm foam pad and run round the edges with the ball tool to re-soften and frill the edges.

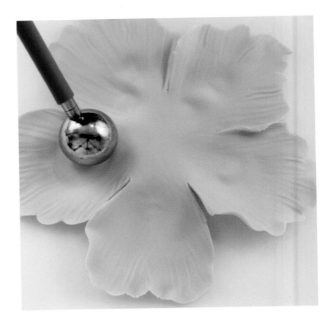

9. Finally, use a larger ball tool to cup each petal slightly by moving the ball tool in little circles in the centre of each petal. This will give a slightly cupped and curved shape that will help form the flower in the next step...

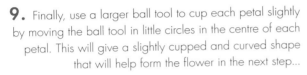

Using the ball tool on the edges a second time fades the veins a little at the ends of the petals, giving a more natural look.

10. Wet the centre and a line up the edges and middle of each petal.

11. Place the petals onto the Rapid Rose pad and insert the prepared peony bud through the centre.

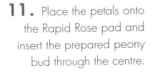

12. Lift a petal up and attach it to the bud, keeping it tight to the bud and curled over - these innermost petals are barely opening yet...

13. Continue adding petals, attaching them to the bud and keeping the tops tight and curled over. There is no particular order in which to attach them - unlike roses, peonies don't have a particular structure being more a jumble of frilly petals!

Unlike making roses with the Rapid Rose pad, you do not need to turn the peony petals over to use them!!

14. Once all the petals are in place, remove the Rapid Rose pad, press the base so the petals are firmly attached and gently curve the tops in to form a tight bud.

15. Cut a second 120mm peony shape and repeat the steps above to prepare the petals. Place on to the Rapid Rose support pad, wet and attach the petals as before, this time placing them so they're a little more open... again there is no particular order to add them.

You can see that the first peony shape inside is curled over tight and the second one a little looser... as if the petals are blooming and opening away from the centre.

16. Having attached all the petals remove the Rapid Rose pad, press the base in and gently adjust the tops of the petals so they are curved over the bud, without being pressed in too tightly.

If you only want to make a small peony bud this is where you can stop. They look great as giant fillers alongside fuller bloomed peonies.

17. Cut a third peony shape with the 120mm cutter. Use the large ball tool, working out from the centre of each petal to make them a little bigger. Follow the steps above to prepare the petals for use.

18. Place your petals onto the Rapid Rose pad, wet as before and attach them... place them less tightly than the last row, so that the petals are opening away from the centre. Flip and press down on the back so everything is firmly attached at the base.

Think about how peonies grow and open: a tight ball of petals which gradually unfurl from the outside...

19. You can use a pokey tool (the 'little spoon' end of the dresden tool is best) to go in gently and re-position the petals so the third row are more open than those inside - you want the petals to cup and curve around the ball shape in the centre. If needs be, allow to dry for a few minutes or so before adding the next row of petals.

20. Cut a fourth peony shape with the 120mm cutter, prepare and attach to your flower as before. Make sure the petals are continuing to 'open' so that the flower increases in size and appears to bloom. Use a pokey tool if you need to nudge the petals out a bit. If needs be allow to dry again for a few minutes before adding the next layer.

21. Insert a drinking straw into a piece of polystyrene. You'll be able put your peony down without having to fight the polystyrene to get it in/out and risking damage!

22. Use the 150mm cutter and follow the same steps above to prepare the petals. Wet and attach the petals as before making sure that they're left fairly open and at an appropriate height in comparison to the inner petals - if this means they're not attached at full height, that's OK as we'll fix it in the next step...

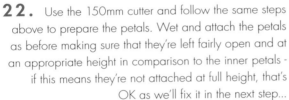

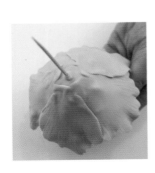

23. Remove the support pad and flip the flower - you may need to press down the wrinkles that have formed from not attaching the petals at their full height. Do this near the base as it won't be visible.

24. Place the peony into the straw/dummy and use your fingers to enhance the shape of the petal tips, making them curl inwards, without squashing them or compacting the whole flower.

25. Tear a piece of kitchen towel into strips, roll them up and place them under the peony to prop up the petals whilst drying. Leave it to dry for at least ten minutes or so before adding the final layer - if you're working in damp or humid conditions it may need a little longer to dry.

26. Cut a final peony shape using the 150mm cutter. Prep the petals and attach as before, this time using them at their full height. If it looks like there is a bit of a gap in the final row, you can cut and add in a single extra petal.

Place back into the straw/dummy and again prop the petals up with rolls of kitchen paper. You can also add some smaller rolls of paper to spread the petals out, tweaking as necessary to get a natural spread and look for the petals.

Sugar peonies are super fine and fragile - make sure it's had plenty of time to dry before dusting or using it on a cake.

SIZES:

Each peony is made with a pair of cutters - the two bigger ones for a large life-sized peony, or the two smaller ones for an overall smaller bloom. It's important to maintain the correct proportion between the central bud and petals, so I don't use all four together as the smallest size requires a bud that would be too small for the biggest petal size to fit around and it would end up looking a bit wrong...

90 & 105mm
Peony Cutters

+ 30mm Poly-Bud
+ 50g flowerpaste
= 8cm Peony

120 & 150mm
Peony Cutters

+ 40mm Poly-Bud
+ 70g flowerpaste
= 11cm Peony

SOME OTHER HINTS AND TIPS:

• The Rapid Rose support pad works best when you hold it firmly - grip the cocktail stick beneath the bud nice and tight so it doesn't move or wobble while you work.

• Sometimes you'll end up with a feathery edge on your petals as a result of the cutter and ball tool. Fear not as these little bits will easily flick off once dry.

• If your paste is a bit floppy, for example because you've added a lot of colouring or the weather is really damp, you may need to let everything dry a bit longer between adding rows of petals... don't rush and risk damaging the flower!

• Remember that nature doesn't grow everything exactly the same, so if some of your petals end up looking a little odd or squiffy don't stress, it'll just add to the realism!

As always, build the layers of colour slowly - you can always add more but once it's on there you can't take it away!

DUSTING:

Use a wide soft brush to apply the petal dust. Keep your strokes light and aim to catch the edges of the petals. Start in the centre working towards the outside of the peony. Use side-to-side motions to colour the curled tops of the petals, highlighting the veins and adding detail.

ADVANCED DUSTING!

For an alternative look you can dust the peony as you make it. This isn't hard to do in terms of dusting, but you do need to work *really* quickly as the dust will dry out the flowerpaste!

This method works really well with paler colours, giving a natural and realistic looking depth to the layers of delicate petals.

Before you start attaching petals, add a little dust to the flowerpaste circle on the top of the poly-ball (Step 4 above).

Continue to create the peony as above, but *before* attaching each row of petals, dust them from the centre towards the edges, so that the colour blooms and spreads out from the centre...

For a deeper, more intense effect, you can also add a little dust to the outside of each row of petals, before adding the next.

FILLER FLOWERS

Filler flowers are wonderful little things, used to add depth and interest
to your designs. They do exactly what the name suggests - fill the space with
flowery goodness! They're an excellent opportunity to add in another colour
or different shade of the same colour, making your design
look more interesting and realistic.

RUFFLE FILLERS - YOU WILL NEED:

- Basic Tools • Set of Hydrangea Cutters • 24g wire, cut to approx. 8cm lengths
- Colours used: ColourSplash Raspberry with SugarFlair Plum dust

1. Knead the flowerpaste well so it's soft and pliable. Roll it out and cut out pairs of hydrangeas - each ruffle flower requires a pair of hydrangeas the same size.

2. Use a ball tool or the end of your rolling pin to thin, soften and slightly frill the edges of the flowers. There is no need to be precise so just go at it with enthusiasm!

3. Once you have a matching pair that's been balled and prepped, brush a dot of water on one and place the other on top, at 90° to the first and press firmly to join. Paint a cross of water on the flower as shown.

I love these little filler flowers! They are completely made up but look undeniably flowery... they're so quick to make, perfect for commercial designs.

This is a fiddly action the first few times you do it but do persevere as these are lovely and quick once you have the knack of making them.

4. Pick up the flower in one hand and balance it on the tip of your thumb and forefinger, folding it almost in half, but not quite...

5. Position the thumb and forefinger of your other hand either side of the first and gently squeeze from both directions.

6. Release your first hand and pinch the bottom of the flower with your second - the squeezing at the base will make the petals bloom and open at the top.

8. Place the ruffle flowers on flower foam to dry - the pinch at the base will fit nicely in the grooves.

You can see the pinch underneath on the one that's upside down - this makes them easy to attach unwired to a cake, using a little royal icing to affix them.

WIRED RUFFLE FLOWERS

1. Make a double folded hook on a piece of wire by folding it over and then folding it once more. Prepare the hydrangea shapes as before, moisten the end of the wire and insert it through the centre.

2. Hold the flowers as before, half folded over and balanced it on your fingertips... Position the wire so the hook is about 3mm above the flowers, letting it dangle down past your fingers.

3. Use your other hand to squeeze just like before, ignoring the wire and pinching the base to make the petals open at the top.

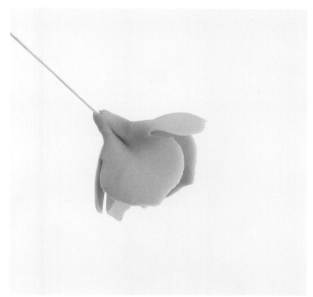

4. Pinch the flowerpaste onto the wire but be careful not to pinch too hard - if you over do it there's a risk of popping the flower up and off the top of the wire. The base won't be visible when you use the flower so don't worry if it's not very neat or pretty; strong is better than pretty! Hang upside down to dry.

DUSTING: Use a wide soft brush to add petal dust in a matching or contrasting colour. Use multiple flicking motions to add the colour to the flower without trying to be precise! The colour will catch the edges of the petals and blend to give you a wonderful two-tone effect.

TIPS FOR RUFFLE FILLERS:

• If you have hydrangea cutters in more than one size then you can make ruffle flowers in more than one size - the bigger the flower the more space it will fill. It's always useful to make a range of sizes so you can fill whatever gaps you end up with... I've even snapped off a couple of petals here and there to make them fit!

• Be careful when you pinch the base closed around a wire - it's so easy to make them pop off the top if you are too rough.

• If you're going to make lots of these, grab a plastic wallet and cut lots at once, placing them in the wallet to keep them from drying. That way you can whizz through dozens in no time at all.

ADDING STAMENS:

Including stamens with these little fillers makes them look even more delightful! Instructions for taping stamens onto the wire can be found later in the this chapter on page 80.

Once you've made your wire with stamens, simply follow the instructions above to make the flower on the wire. Make sure you start the folding action around the wire, not the stamens - as there isn't a double folded hook on the end you need to be extra gentle and careful to not over squeeze and pop the flower off the top.

HYDRANGEA - YOU WILL NEED:

- Basic Tools • Set of Hydrangea Cutters & Mould • 24g wire, cut to approx. 8cm lengths
- Colours used: ColourSplash Raspberry with Squires Pink and SugarFlair Plum dust

1. Take a piece of 24g wire and moisten the top. Roll a tiny cone of flowerpaste and place it onto the end of the wire.

2. Pinch and twist the bottom of the ball down the wire for a neat finish.

3. Use a knife or dresden tool to carefully mark a cross on the top of the flowerpaste blob. Place aside to dry, overnight if possible.

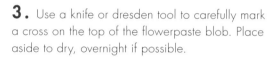

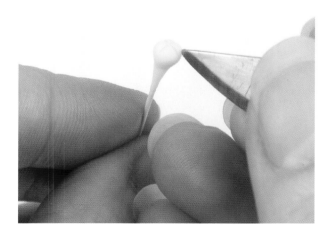

The more of these you make the quicker they become and the easier it will be to make them nice and small.

4. Knead your flowerpaste, roll a ball and pinch one side to make a cone shape.

5. Insert the tip of the cone into a medium sized hole on the mexican hat mat and press down very firmly. You'll want to dust or grease your fingers so you don't stick!

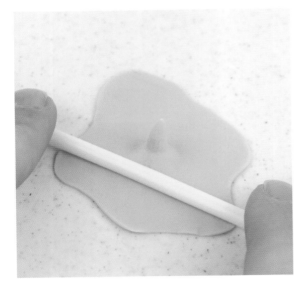

Now do you see why it's called the mexican hat method? Who knew!?!

6. You should end up with a shape that looks a little like a mexican hat, or like one of those old fashioned mushroom sweeties! Place it point up on your workboard and use a cakepop stick as a tiny rolling pin to roll out and thin the paste around the point.

7. Place your cutter on the paste so the point is in the centre and press firmly to cut the hydrangea. I find it easier to pull the flower out backwards by holding onto the point, than to push it through.

8. Place the hydrangea onto the mould and press the petals down with your fingers - don't try to close the mould! The top of the mould is the side where the centre is a dip.

9. Once veined, place the hydrangea back into a *bigger* hole on the mexican-hat mat (so it doesn't get stuck!). Use a small ball tool to thin and slightly frill the edge of each petal.

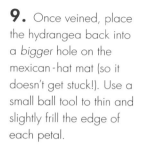

10. Take the prepared centre and moisten the stem with a little water. Carefully insert the wire and pull it down so that the centre sits just above the surface of the flower.

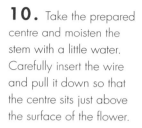

11. Pinch the paste around the stem and twist it round to remove the excess for a neat finish. Be careful not to pinch upwards as you'll pop the flower off the top of the wire.

12. Once the flower is firmly attached to the wire, use a knife to carefully cut a small slit in between each petal - this will free the petals from one another a little and thus allow a little more freedom and movement.

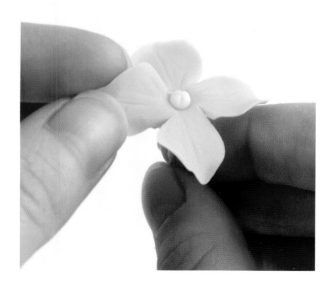

As there are a few steps to making the wired hydrangea it's important to start with fresh, well kneaded paste so it doesn't dry out too much before you've finished...

13. Carefully twist and shape each petal, curling them up to give the hydrangea a more natural looking shape. Hang upside down to dry.

DUSTING:

Once dry, use a soft small brush to add some petal dust to the edges, giving definition to each petal. I also like to darken the centre a little bit, using a small pointed brush to add just a little colour.

Hydrangea grow in a wide range of colours, from deep pinks and purples to blues, whites and greens... they're a great flower to experiment and practice with colours and petal dusts.

UN-WIRED HYDRANGEA

1. Cut the required size from thinly rolled flower paste. Apply a little corn flour to both sides of the mould so the flowerpaste doesn't stick. Place the hydrangea in the centre of the mould, fold over and press firmly.

2. Put the flower on the firm foam pad and use a small ball tool to thin and shape the edges.

3. Use a blade tool or dresden/veiner to press down in between each petal. Don't press too hard as you don't want to cut the paste, but you do want to make enough of an impression that the petals look more defined.

4. Put the hydrangea onto the flower foam to dry. Press the centre down into the hole a little so the petals are forced up and the hydrangea take on a more natural shape. Once dry, dust in the same way as the wired hydrangea.

CALYX FLOWERS - YOU WILL NEED:

- Basic Tools • Calyx Cutters • 24g wire, cut to approx. 8cm lengths
- Small White Stamens • White Floral Tape
- Colours used: ColourSplash Burgundy with Squires Pink dust

1. Cut the tape to quarter width and the tiny stamens in half...

Attaching stamens to wire is a fiddly job, but worth the effort as they look so pretty and delicate!

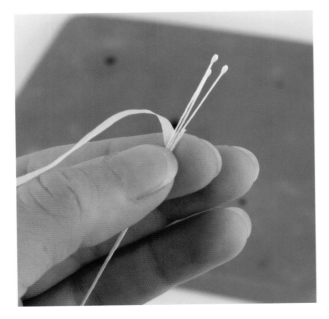

2. Take a piece of wire and attach the tape about 4cm from the top, winding it upwards... take two or three stamens, place them with the top of the wire overlapping by approx. 4mm and hold them tight between your thumb and forefinger as shown.

3. Wrap the tape round both the wire and the stamens, extending the tape a little above the end of the wire and then bringing it back down past the end of the stamens so the join and stem is smooth.

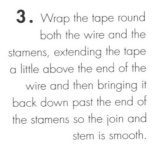

4. As for the hydrangea on the previous pages, make a mexican hat and use the cake pop stick to roll it thinner.

5. Place the calyx cutter over the stem and press firmly to cut. It can be easier to pull the flower out by the stem than to push it out as you normal would. If needs be, a gentle prod with a small ball tool from the front will help release the flower.

6. Place the flower into a bigger hole on the mexican hat pad and use a small ball tool to soften and elongate the petals. Move the ball tool from the centre and then up and out for each petal, so the motion follows the way the petals grow.

This is not necessarily what Calyx cutters are designed for... but these little flowers are so cute and delicate. Despite being made up they look something akin to a jasmine or stephanotis.

Be very gentle when performing these steps, the flowers are delicate and it's easy to accidentally damage or tear a petal!

7. Use a star tool to gently press into the centre of the flower, making a little dip and adding detail. Don't press too hard or you risk making a hole or weak point where the paste is squashed between the mexican hat pad and the star tool.

8. Moisten the end of the wire, just below the stamens and insert it into the centre of the flower, pulling the flower up the wire.

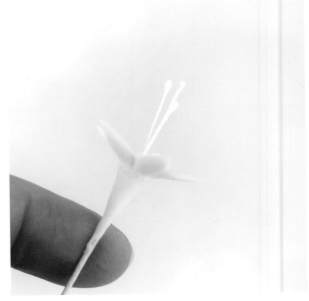

9. Once the flower is in position, gently pinch the stem around the wire. Twist it in between your thumb and forefinger to twiddlle the paste down the wire for a neat finish, removing any excess. Be careful and gentle as it's easy to damage the flower or push it too far up the wire/stamens.

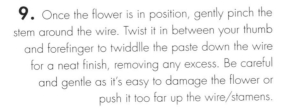

10. Use your fingers to pinch the ends of the petals into a point and shape the petals - I tend to curl them upwards a little, as if the flower is blooming.

Depending upon how dry your paste is and the climate you are working in, these may need hanging upside down to dry so the petals don't flop backwards. They're super fragile so let them dry completely before doing anything else with them.

DUSTING:

To finish them off, add a tiny amount of petal dust to the very centre of the flower with a pointed brush, drawing just a little colour up the centre of each petal. I like to leave these pale and super delicate looking, adding just the teeniest amount of dust in a similar colour.

If your colour palette includes metallics these look fabulous with the stamens painted, adding just a hint of shiny gold or silver...

LEAVES

Leaves are one of my favourite things to make and dust.
Adding lush green leaves to flowers always makes everything look
fresher and more alive. Don't get too hung up on the type of leaf
you're using - it's just greenery and you can always change
and amend the colour to suit your design and
match the flowers.

ROSE LEAVES - YOU WILL NEED:

- Basic Tools • Rose Leaf Cutter • Rose Leaf Veiner
- 28g wire, cut to approx. 8cm lengths
- Colours used: Squires Leaf with Squires Leaf Green, Fractal Olive and RainbowDust Claret dusts

1. Roll out your flowerpaste so that it's thicker at one end than the other... do this by increasing the pressure as you roll away from yourself, so that the bit nearest to you remains a little thicker than the rest. (This is so that we have a thicker bit in which to place the wire.)

If you're making lots of leaves, this little trick of rolling one end of the flowerpaste thicker will save loads of time!

2. Cut out a leaf, making sure that the base of the leaf is at the thicker end of the flowerpaste.

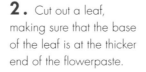

3. Place the leaf onto the firm foam pad and use a ball tool to soften and thin the edges of the leaf: sweep up each side of the leaf, base to top, following the direction that the leaf grows.

Using the ball tool like this means that the leaf will be stretched and shaped in a natural looking way...

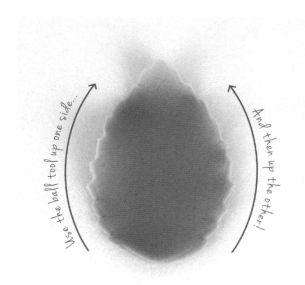

Use the ball tool up one side...

And then up the other!

4. Wet the end of the wire with a little water, hold the leaf between your forefinger and thumb in one hand and with the other carefully insert the wire about 1/3 to 1/2 way up - your finger and thumb will be able to feel it inside the paste; you'll know if you've gone wrong!

5. Pinch the base of the leaf closed around the wire, being careful not to damage the leaf or let the wire poke through.

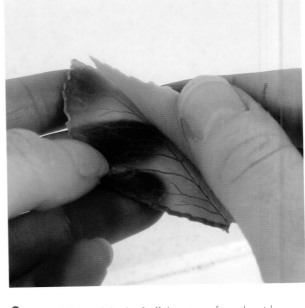

6. Give your veiner a very light dusting of cornflour...

7. Place the veiner onto the leaf and press firmly all over the leaf...

Put the leaf onto a hard surface to press in the veiner so you get a clear, deep impression

8. Carefully peel the leaf off the veiner from the side - don't try to pull it off by the wire as you will likely tear the flowerpaste and/or pull the wire out!

9. Put the leaf back onto the firm foam pad and go round the edge once more with a ball tool to put some shape back into the leaf and to fade out the veins just a little, so they don't stop dead at the edges.

10. Place the leaves onto some drying foam, having given each one a little twist or flick so they dry with a dynamic shape, rather than flat and rigid.

It can be useful to make a few unwired leaves - these can be stuck directly on to a cake or used to droop over the side of a tier...

... think about the design of the finished cake as you make the leaves and dry them accordingly.

A SLIGHTLY BIGGER LEAF:

If you want to make a slightly bigger leaf you can roll out the flowerpaste thicker than you normally would and use a ball tool to stretch it out:

• Run the ball tool up the centre to make it longer
• Then from the centre out towards the left and to the right
• And then proceed as normal from Step 3 to make and vein the leaf..

DUSTING: Leaves look best if the colour is applied in layers, so they are not just one flat shade of green. Depending upon your base colour, you can follow these same steps with a range of lighter or darker colours to make lighter or darker leaves.

1. Start with a fully dry flowerpaste leaf...

2. Use a wide flat brush to apply a dust that more-or-less matches the flowerpaste colour. This will intensify the base colour and act as a 'carrier' for the other dusts.

3. Dust around the edges with a darker green. Use short flicking motions going from the outside to towards the centre to blend the dusts and make a smooth colour gradient, whilst also giving an 'outline' the edge of the rose leaf.

4. Finally, on just some of the leaves, add a touch of something from the red family of colours ie. reds, browns or pinks. Mixed with the greens this will give the look of a leaf that's on the turn - just as rose leaves often are!

Add the colour slowly - you can always add more but you cannot take it away!

TAPING: Rose leaves grow symmetrically in pairs, directly opposite each other on the branch...
I don't much like how that looks for sugar flowers, so I tend to tape them into little branches or sprigs that
aren't symmetrical. These little sprigs are useful 'ready to use' units, prepared for placing on your cake.

SMALL SPRIGS: Simply
tape two or three leaves
together at a time. Vary the
height and size of the leaves
to add interest and give a
more dynamic look.

LARGE SPRIGS: For a little branch of rose leaves, start with the
smallest and attach the tape. Wind it down a little and then attach
a leaf of the next size... wind it down a little more and attach
another leaf on the opposite side. Continue until your branch is as
large as required.

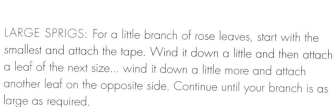

These leafy branches are gorgeous little things to make, but do require a little extra planning so that you've made the right number of leaves to tape together...

The Foliage Allsorts tappit comes with a left and a right cutter.
Each side has six sizes of leaf - I'm going to call the smallest leaf
No.1, running through the sizes with No. 6 being the biggest...
(I tend not to use size No.1 as it's so very very tiny.)

Here's a branch laid out, showing which
sizes you need and in what order:

No. 3, Left

No. 4, Left

Size No.2
(left or right)

No. 5, Left

No. 3, Right

No. 6, Left

No. 4, Right

No. 5, Right

No. 6, Right

As you can see you will need the right number of each size, left and/or
right, to be able to build a branch. If you wanted a longer branch you
could do two of each size, or for a shorter branch skip one of the sizes...
it'll work so long as you have matching pairs of left and right leaves.

LEAFY BRANCHES - YOU WILL NEED:

- Basic Tools • Foliage Allsorts Tappit • 28g wire, cut to approx. 8cm lengths
- Colours used: Squires Leaf and RainbowDust Lime with EdAbleArt Kiwi and Fractal Olive dusts

1. Roll out your flowerpaste so that it's thicker at one end than the other... Press the tappit onto the flowerpaste so that the base of the leaf is at the thicker end. Press firmly and give it a wiggle to cut.

2. Place the tappit over the edge of your firm foam pad and flick the end so that the leaf is released.

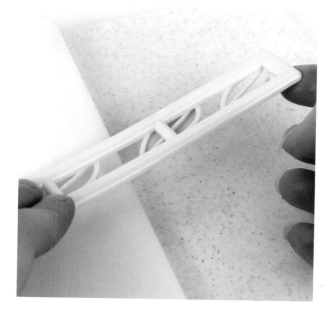

3. Use a ball tool to lightly soften the edges of the leaf, running it base to tip on each side.

4. Wet the end of the wire with a little water, hold the leaf between your forefinger and thumb in one hand and with the other carefully insert the wire about 1/3 to 1/2 way up the leaf.

5. Pinch the base closed around the wire, being careful not to damage the leaf or poke the wire through.

6. Make as many leaves as required for your branch by repeating the steps above and lay them to dry with a little twist or flick...

I find it's really helpful if you lay the little leaves out as you make them so you can see what you've made and how many more are needed to complete the branch.

DUSTING: For these little leafy branches I like to dust them darker at the base - when taped together this gives a beautiful effect, with the colour spreading up and out and from the centre of the branch.

1. Apply a little dust all over to intensify the base colour

2. Apply a darker colour from the base up. Use short flicking motions so that the colours are blended and smooth...

TAPING: Once you have the right number of leaves in the right sizes, these are pretty easy to tape together. The most important thing is to leave a bigger gap in between each leaf as the leaves themselves get bigger; this will maintain the proportions so that you create a branch, rather than something like a fern or palm frond.

1. Attach the tape to the first leaf and wind it down around 2.5cm or so.

2. Bend the wire of the second leaf, hold it in place and wrap the tape around both wires to attach it.

3. Wind the tape down again, making a big enough gap that the third leaf will sit in the right place...

4. Wrap the tape around to attach the leaf, and again wind it down a little further than before, so there is enough space for the next, bigger leaf...

5. Repeat as above, creating gaps of increasing size so that there is space for the larger leaves and the branch has a natural look, as if it's growing!

Remember that as each of the leaves is wired, you can bend both the branch as a whole and each leaf, adding shape and movement to your arrangements.

SMALL SPRIGS: To add texture and interest to your floral work, the larger of these leaves can be taped together into sprigs of two, three or four at a time. They're a nice change from rose leaves and make great fillers. You can either tape them together in one go or one-by-one to make a sort of 'mini'-branch.

PEONY LEAVES - YOU WILL NEED:

- Basic Tools • Cutting Wheel • 26g wire, cut to approx. 8cm lengths
- Colours used: Squires Holly/Ivy with Fractal Olive and RainbowDust Moss Green dusts

1. Roll out your flowerpaste so that it's thicker at one end than the other... Using a cutting wheel, cut out a leaf shape (see page 98 for a guide on getting the right shapes).

2. Place the leaf onto your firm foam pad and run round the edges with a ball tool to soften them and give the leaf a little shape.

3. Use the dresden tool to give the leaf long vertical veins as shown. Do this on the foam pad as it's less likely that you will press too hard and accidentally split the leaf.

4. Wet the end of the wire with a little water, hold the leaf between your forefinger and thumb in one hand and with the other carefully insert the wire about 1/3 to 1/2 way up.

5. Pinch the base of the leaf closed around the wire, being careful not to damage the leaf or let the wire poke through.

6. Place them onto the flower foam to dry, arranging them with a little twist or flick to add some movement.

Like rose leaves, it can also be useful to make some unwired peony leaves, to stick directly onto the cake or use to droop over the side of a tier - think about how you plan to use them as you make them...

CUTTING GUIDE:

The leaves we need for this are a pretty basic shape. I tend to cut some fatter and some thinner for a little variation, the length depending upon the size and shape of the arrangement/flowers that they're going to go with... To pair with a large peony I make them around 6 - 9 cm long and for a small peony, around 4 - 6 cm long.

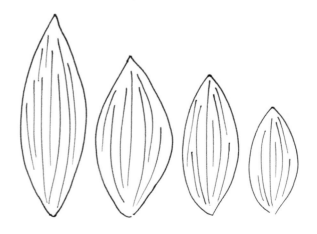

DUSTING:

I like to keep it simple for dusting peony leaves: use a wide soft brush to dust all over with a similar shade of green to intensify the colour and then add a few streaks of darker green, from base to tip.

Peony leaves actually grow with multiple fingers on each leaf. Making them like this and taping them together is quicker, easier and means that they are far less fragile and less likely to break!

TAPING: Tape the leaves into little bunches of two or three, varying the height and bending the wires to give the bunches shape and life. These will make useful little units, ready to place on a cake.

BUDS AND BERRIES

Simple, cute and quick to create, buds and berries make excellent
fillers and are a really great way to add a little pop of contrasting
colour or texture - think lime green berries alongside pink
roses or textured seed pods amongst crisp white roses.
It's those little details which will bring your work to life
and add a great deal of realism..

BASIC BERRIES - YOU WILL NEED:

- Basic Tools • 28g wire, cut to approx. 8cm lengths • A tealight candle
- Colours used: ColourSplash Raspberry with SugarFlair Plum dust

1. Knead your flowerpaste and roll a small ball of paste, around the size of a petit-pois or garden pea.

2. Light the tealight and hold the wire in the flame to heat it up. If the paper catches light, quickly remove it from the flame so it doesn't burn all the way down the wire, and then begin heating it again.

3. Once the wire is red-hot, quickly insert it into the berry. You should see a puff of smoke and it will smell like burnt sugar...

Be careful with the open flame - mind your hair and hands if you lean over to reach for things... I speak from experience!

4. If you find that the tape burns too far down the wire, don't worry! When you insert the wire, simply push the berry on far enough that the burnt part is covered. Once they've had a little while to dry you can then snip the ends off with a pair of wire cutters.

I make berries this way as it's so quick - having heated the wire, the berries will be firmly attached and ready to use in a couple of hours.

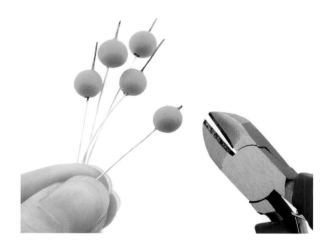

DUSTING: The final flourish to finish the berries is to add a little petal dust - I like to use the same colour as the flowerpaste, but in a darker shade. Use a soft brush about 1cm wide, applying the dust to the base of the berry and up one side to give a greater depth of colour and add some shading. You can then use floral tape to tape them together into little clusters of two, three, four or five berries, ready for use.

GLORIOUS GLAZES

Edible glaze can be painted on to make berries super shiny. These red berries look so lush and realistic - set alongside matt red roses they give life and texture to an arrangement without adding in extra colours.

MARVELLOUS METALLICS

Berries are also an excellent way to add a metallic highlight to a design, giving just a hint of gold, silver or bronze. Mix a fairly thick paint by combining metallic lustre dust and rejuvenator spirit, using a soft brush to apply it to the berries. Once they are dry, give them a light spray with an edible glaze spray to fix the paint.

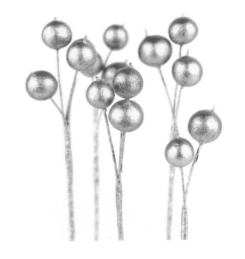

THE LEGUME SCALE:

I've made a habit of describing the size of berries and buds in reference to the size of peas. Here's my official legume scale of sizes:

Petit-Pois   Garden Pea   Chickpea   Large Chickpea

BASIC BUDS - YOU WILL NEED:

- Basic Tools • 28g wire, cut to approx. 8cm lengths • A tealight candle
- Colours used: ColourSplash Burgundy with Squires Pink and SugarFlair Plum dust

1. Using the flowerpaste, make a small tear drop shape by forming a ball and then rolling one side of it between your thumb and forefinger, to give a pointed end.

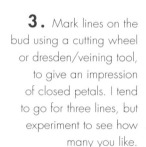

2. Carefully heat the wire in the candle flame, trying to avoid burning too much of the paper. Insert into the bud and pinch the base closed around the wire.

3. Mark lines on the bud using a cutting wheel or dresden/veining tool, to give an impression of closed petals. I tend to go for three lines, but experiment to see how many you like.

Vary the size and shape of the buds: thin ones in different sizes will make a cute branch of buds or make them fatter to tape into clusters.

DUSTING: To finish the buds, I like to use a dust that's a little darker than the flowerpaste. Use a soft, flat brush to gently apply the colour from the bottom up, giving a slightly darker base to the bud.

TAPING: To make a little branch of buds, attach the tape to your first one and then wind it down the stem a little... bend the next bud over a wee bit, hold it alongside and wrap the tape around both to attach it to the original bud...

...Continue adding buds in the same way to make a small branch - I tend use between three and six per branch and they look even better if you start with slightly smaller buds at the top, increasing in size as you move down the branch.

FAT BUDS: For an alternative look, try making the buds a bit chunkier and fatter at the base - about the size of a large chickpea. Mark the lines in the same way and dust them to be darker at the bottom. These look really good taped into clusters of two or three and make an excellent filler for your arrangements. I particularly like them made in shades of bright green - they look so alive and fresh!

SEED PODS - YOU WILL NEED:

- 24g wire, cut to approx. 8cm lengths • A tealight candle and lighter • Tweezers
- Colours used: SugarFlair Grape with SugarFlair African Violet and RainbowDust Shadow Grey dust

1. Roll a ball about the size of a large chickpea. Heat the wire, insert it and twiddle the base of the ball onto the wire. As the wire is thicker than that used for the berries it will take longer to heat up.

2. Before the flowerpaste starts to set, use a pair of tweezers to pinch the paste at odd and differing angles, all over the ball.

Made in more natural shades of brown or green, these make an excellent addition to rustic or botanical designs.

DUSTING: Once dry, dust with a similar or slightly darker shade to intensify the colour. I then like to use a soft brush with a different colour in soft broad sweeps to catch the ridges, giving a two-tone look to the pods. Experiment with the colours as unusual combos can produce some really interesting looking results!

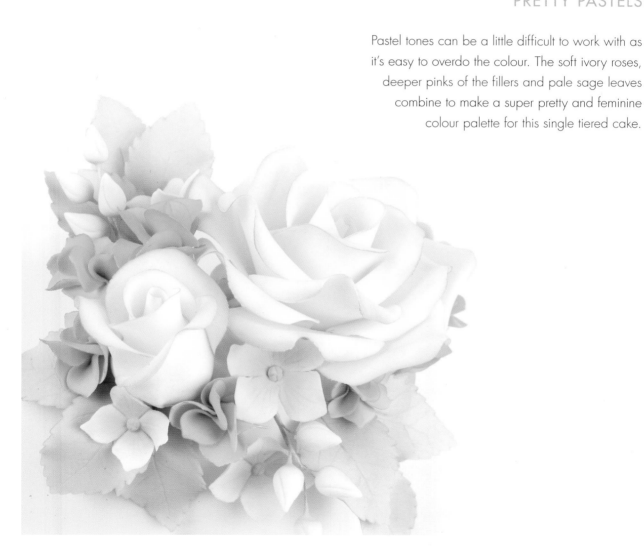

Project One

PRETTY PASTELS

Pastel tones can be a little difficult to work with as it's easy to overdo the colour. The soft ivory roses, deeper pinks of the fillers and pale sage leaves combine to make a super pretty and feminine colour palette for this single tiered cake.

YOU WILL NEED:

- CAKE 6" round x 5" tall
  Covered with pale pink sugarpaste
  (ColourSplash Burgundy)

- TOOLS
  Pliers & wire cutters, posy picks,
  some leftover sugarpaste and
  a small bag of royal icing.

- ROSES
  1 x full rose with 12cm cutter
  1 x rose bud with 10cm cutter

- BUDS
  Approx. 10, to make
  two small branches

- HYDRANGEA
  5 x wired hydrangea, mix of sizes
  5 x unwired hydrangea, mix of sizes

- RUFFLE FILLERS
  8 x wired, mix of sizes
  5 x unwired, mix of sizes

- ROSE LEAVES
  8 x wired, mix of medium and large
  5 x unwired, large and dried to
  droop over the edge of the cake

The quantities on the list allow for a couple spare, just in case you need extra when arranging or if something gets broken!

COLOURS:

IVORY
PEACH
PINK
SAGE

RUFFLE FILLERS - approx. 45g flowerpaste

SugarFlair: ColourSplash: Pale Pink
Grape   Burgundy

ROSES - approx. 90g flowerpaste

ColourSplash: SugarFlair: Palest Peach
Burgundy   Egg Yellow

LEAVES - approx. 45g flowerpaste

RainbowDust: RainbowDust: Pale Tealy Sage
Grey   Eucalyptus

BUDS & HYDRANGEA - approx. 50g flowerpaste

Palest Peach   ColourSplash: Pale Peachy
(see above)   Burgundy   Pink

DUSTS:

RainbowDust:
Pale Terracotta

Squires:
Pink

SugarFlair:
Fuchsia

EdAbleArt:
Eucalyptus

Even though these dusts look bright, we're only going to use a very tiny amount, adding the colour slowly to achieve pale and pastel tones.

Use a wide soft brush to apply the pale terracotta to the edges of the roses. Add just a tiny amount of pink to the edges to deepen the colour and add interest.

Dust from the edges towards the centre with eucalyptus. This will define the edges and highlight the veins.

Mix some pink with just a little fuchsia to make a brighter pink. Use a small brush to apply the colour to the middle of the hydrangea, drawing a little colour up each petal.

Mix the pink and fuchsia again, adding a little more fuchsia for a brighter pink. Use a wide soft brush to apply the dust all over the ruffle fillers.

Apply a little pink to the base of the buds, drawing the colour upwards so it fades out...

ARRANGING:

Tape the buds together into a couple of little branches and make two small sprigs of rose leaves. All the other bits can remain loose as this will give you more options when arranging them onto the cake.

It's always best to start with the largest flowers as the rest of the design will be formed around this focal point.

Begin by positioning the roses - we want the larger rose to sit a little higher than the rose bud. Simply insert it through a blob of fondant to raise it up.

Insert a posy pick just
behind the roses and fill
it with a little sausage of
sugarpaste.

Place the first sprig of rose leaves into the
posy pick along with a branch of buds and
some ruffle fillers. Bend and shape the wires
so that they appear natural and dynamic.

Take a couple of the unwired leaves and attach
them to the cake under the roses, using a
little royal icing to attach them.

Use a little water
to affix a blob of
sugarpaste in between
the roses, squashing
it into place with a
pokey tool...

Insert another sprig of rose leaves and branch of buds into the blob of sugarpaste.

Add some filler flowers, having cut the wires short, to build up the area beneath the roses. The lowest hydrangea is unwired and has been attached to the side of the cake with royal icing.

Continue adding fillers and leaves to bulk out the arrangement... the fillers to the right of the roses have been poked into the sugarpaste that's holding the rose up and there are a couple extra unwired leaves and fillers that have been attached directly onto the cake.

The sweet soft colours of this design would look beautiful on a wedding cake - you could use these colours with the design from Project Three.

Project Two

SUNNY BLUES

Combining sunny yellows with blues and a deep tealy green makes for a bright, yet mature, combination of colours. The pale grey background is soft and subtle, giving an overall elegant feel to this modern design.

YOU WILL NEED:

- CAKE 6" round x 4.5" tall
        8" round x 5.5" tall
  Covered with pale grey
  sugarpaste (RainbowDust Grey)

- TOOLS
  Pliers & wire cutters, posy picks,
  some leftover sugarpaste and
  a small bag of royal icing.

- PEONIES
  1 x full large peony
  1 x large peony bud

- BERRIES
  Approx. 12 on white wires

- RUFFLE FILLERS
  10 x wired ruffles, mix of sizes

- SEED PODS
  Approx. 10

- PEONY LEAVES
  6 x wired, mix of medium
  and large
  5 x unwired, large and dried
  to droop over the edge
  of the cake

- LEAFY BRANCHES
  10 leaves of the three
  largest sizes,enough
  to make two
  small branches

With a relatively short list of flowers
to make, this design is quick to
do but very effective!

COLOURS:

YELLOW
BLUE
GREY
NAVY
GREEN

PEONIES & BERRIES - approx. 100g flowerpaste

 + =

RainbowDust:
Yellow

SugarFlair:
Egg Yellow

Sunny Yellow

RUFFLE FILLERS - approx. 40g flowerpaste

 + =

Wilton:
Royal Blue

SugarFlair:
Grape

Cornflower Blue

LEAVES - approx. 45g flowerpaste

 + =

RainbowDust:
Green

Wilton:
Christmas Red

Deep Green

SEED PODS - approx. 25g flowerpaste

 + =

Wilton:
Royal Blue

SugarFlair:
Grape

Deep Navy

DUSTS:

RainbowDust:
Shadow Grey

RainbowDust:
Royal Blue

Squires:
Marigold

EdAbleArt:
Tangerine

EdAbleArt:
Teal

RainbowDust:
Navy

Dust the peonies as you make them with the marigold dust, using the advanced method described on page 67.

Dust the berries with marigold and just a hint of tangerine to make them bright and sunny.

Mix the royal blue and grey to make a muted blue and dust all over the ruffles.

Dust the leaves all over with teal, to intensify the colour and give a very slight tealy-blue tinge to the green.

Dust the seed pods with the navy to give a deep, rich colour. Add a tiny bit royal blue to lift and highlight some of the ridges.

ARRANGING:

Tape the small leaves into a couple of branches and sprigs as shown. Tape the berries and seed pods into bunches. Leave everything else loose as this will give you more options when building the arrangement.

Be very gentle when placing the peonies on the cake, they're very fragile and it's easy to chip or break a petal.

Begin by inserting the larger peony first, then the peony bud. Use thin-nosed pliers to grip the cocktail stick and push it into the cake - don't put any pressure on the petals or front of the flowers! Think about the angle of the flowers in relation to the front of the cake and how it will be viewed.

Use a little water to affix a blob of fondant behind and in between the peonies - this will help to hold them in place and give us somewhere to insert leaves, fillers etc...

Attach a few of the unwired peony leaves under the peonies, using a little royal icing to affix them in place.

Push a posy pick into the cake, just behind the largest peony. Fill it with sugarpaste and place a couple of peony leaves and a branch in it. Place the second branch in the sugarpaste blob under the peonies.

Start filling out the design with the berries, seed pods and filler flowers, placing them into the sugarpaste blobs or posy pick as necessary. You can always enlarge a blob or add another if needs be.

Continue to add the fillers, thinking about placement and distribution of colour as you go so that the arrangement looks well spaced and natural.

Remember that as your fillers and leaves are on wires they can be bent and twisted into pleasing and natural shapes

I love this colour combo, but also think this simple and striking design would also look great in a bright pink or peach...

Project Three

TROPICAL DELIGHT

The intense pinks, corals and limes on this cake make for a bright and tropical looking colour palette. The background colour is ivory - it's a little softer than bright white and the yellowish tones match beautifully with the colourful flowers.

YOU WILL NEED:

- CAKE 5" round x 5" tall
  7" round x 5" tall
  9" round x 5" tall
  Covered with ivory sugarpaste

- TOOLS
  Pliers & wire cutters, posy picks,
  some leftover sugarpaste and a
  small bag of royal icing.

- HYDRANGEA
  10 x wired, mix of sizes
  6 x unwired, mix of sizes

- CALYX FILLERS
  10 x with white stamens,
  mostly small, with a few
  a little bigger.

- BERRIES
  Approx. 25 on green wires

- BUDS
  12 x peach to make
  branches, various sizes
  10 x pale green, fat buds

- SEED PODS
  Approx. 7 - 10

- ROSE LEAVES
  12 x wired, mix of
  medium and large
  8 x unwired, large and dried to
  droop over the edge of the cake

- LEAFY BRANCHES
  18 x leaves to make two
  branches (see page 96)
  6 x largest two sizes to make
  extra sprigs

- ROSES
  1 x full 12cm rose
  1 x small 10cm rose
  (finished with two rows of five)
  1 x full 9cm rose
  2 x small 9cm rose

- RUFFLE FILLERS
  18 x wired, mix of sizes
  12 x unwired, mix of sizes

COLOURS:

LIMES
CORAL
PINK
MAGENTA

ROSES - approx. 300g flowerpaste

ColourSplash: SugarFlair: Rosy Pink
Raspberry   Grape

RUFFLE FILLERS - approx. 50g flowerpaste

ColourSplash: ColourSplash: Bright Coral
Raspberry   Orange

HYDRANGEA - approx. 30g flowerpaste

Rosy Pink   ColourSplash: Magenta
(See above)   Raspberry

PEACH BUDS - approx. 15g flowerpaste

ColourSplash: ColourSplash: Pale Peach
Raspberry   Orange

LEAVES - approx. 50g flowerpaste

RainbowDust:
Lime

+

ColourSplash:
Orange

=

Limey Khaki

SEED PODS - approx. 20g flowerpaste

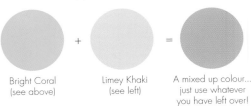

Bright Coral
(see above)

+

Limey Khaki
(see left)

=

A mixed up colour...
just use whatever
you have left over!

BERRIES - approx.
15g flowerpaste

RainbowDust:
Lime

LIME BUDS - approx.
15g flowerpaste

RainbowDust:
Lime

CALYX FILLERS - approx.
30g flowerpaste

ColourSplash:
Raspberry

DUSTS:

SugarFlair:
Fuchsia

SugarFlair:
Plum

Squires:
Pink

Squires:
Leaf Green

EdAbleArt:
Kiwi

RainbowDust:
Citrus Green

Use a wide brush to dust
all over with the fuchsia.
This will catch the
edges, intensifying the
colour and making them
look a little pinker.

Mix a little plum and
fuchsia together to make
an intense, bright pink.
Use a small brush to dust
the centre of the hydrangea
and around the edges.

Use a small brush to apply just a little pink to the centre of the calyx flowers.

Dust the base of the green buds with citrus; for the peach buds use a little fuchsia.

Mix some fuchsia and plum to make a bright pink and dust the edges of the rose petals, using a wide soft brush.

Dust all over the rose leaves with the citrus green and add some leaf green on the edges and base. On some of the leaves use just a touch of the plum or fuchsia to darken the edge.

Dust the berries with the kiwi to make them bright, focusing on the base to give a little colour variation.

Dust all over with the citrus green and then use a little kiwi, followed by the leaf green, to darken the base and achieve a nice smooth gradient.

Dust the pods with fuchsia all over and then use short flicking motions with the greens to catch the ridges. These are not precise - have a play with the colours!

ARRANGING:

Create two branches and a couple of sprigs with the small leaves. Tape the berries and green buds into clusters. Make a couple of branches with the peach buds and a few sprigs with the rose leaves. Everything else can stay untaped, giving more options for arranging them on the cake.

Make a dome of sugarpaste on the top of your cake. It won't be seen in the end so it doesn't need to be perfect.

Start by placing the 12cm and 10cm roses into the dome. Think about where the front of the cake will be so that they're placed at a pleasing angle for the viewer.

Use a little royal icing to attach some unwired leaves under the roses. Bend the stem of one of the branches and insert it into the sugarpaste dome.

Start adding filler flowers, leaves, buds and berries. Be mindful of where the front is so that it looks best from that angle. Think about the colours and building an even, balanced spread.

Continue building up the front of the cake, adding fillers etc. behind, beside and under the roses. For anything low down you can always use unwired items and royal icing, affixing them to the sides or top of the cake.

Insert the full 9cm rose into the top of the bottom tier. Think about placement and where the front of the cake is, so that you place it at the right angle, in the right position.

Sugarpaste is so useful when arranging flowers, the blobs will dry hard and hold everything in place...

We want the smaller 9cm rose to sit a little higher than the full one, so insert it through a lump of sugarpaste to raise it up.

Attach a couple of unwired leaves underneath the roses. If needs be, you can use a small ball of sugarpaste to make the leaves sit a little proud of the side of the cake.

Insert a posy pick just behind the smaller rose, and fill it with a sausage of sugarpaste.

Insert the second leafy branch into the posy pick, along with some rose leaves, buds, pods and calyx fillers.

Attach a small blob of fondant beside the larger rose and insert some leaves, berries and calyx fillers....

Continue adding fillers, leaves, berries, buds and seed pods...

As you add the different elements, think about colour and position so that you create a well balanced design with pleasing shapes.

Now that we've finished the front of the cake and everything looks good, turn to the back. Place the final small rose and use the remaining fillers, leaves, buds and berries to fill the space.

To finish, add a couple of fillers and leaves at the bottom, using royal icing to hold them in place. It doesn't much matter which you choose and if you've only wired items left you can just chop the wire off!

A LAST MINUTE ADJUSTMENT:

Having finished the cake, I stood back to take a good look at it and something wasn't quite right: the leafy branch on the top tier. It drooped down just a little bit too far!

Before doing anything drastic I bent the last leaf out the way and rearranged the others (pictured) and decided it looked much better... so I carefully snipped the wire and removed the leaf.

Yours may look OK, or there may be something else that you decide to change. Either way it's all good - each cake will be slightly different as the flowers are all different... With everything being handmade it's inevitable!

Sorry tiny leaf!

This is a wonderfully versatile wedding design that can be adapted for four tiers and would look great in any colour scheme - experiment and enjoy the process!

SUPPLIERS

The tools and supplies used throughout this book are available from specialist sugarcraft and cake decorating shops.

Those suppliers and manufacturers named within the book can be found below:

NATALIE PORTER'S IMMACULATE CONFECTIONS
www.immaculateconfections.co.uk

BLOSSOM SUGAR ART
www.blossomsugarart.com

FMM SUGARCRAFT
www.fmmsugarcraft.com

SQUIRE'S KITCHEN
www.squires-shop.com

RAINBOW DUST COLOURS
www.rainbowdust.co.uk

EDABLE ART
www.edableartworldofcolour.co.uk

FRACTAL COLORS
www.fractalcolors.com

SUGARFLAIR COLOURS
www.sugarflair.com

WILTON
www.wilton.com

COLOURSPLASH
Available from any good sugarcraft retailer

ISBN: 978-1-9160580-0-2 (Hardback) ISBN: 978-1-9160580-1-9 (eBook)

Published by Portermott Publishing, a trading name of Immaculate Confections Limited www.immaculateconfections.co.uk

ABOUT THE AUTHOR

Natalie Porter is the owner of
Immaculate Confections, based
in South-East England.

She started making cakes in 2012
and has since developed a successful
business. In 2014 she took the
plunge and entered the prestigious
Cake International competitions,
winning Gold for her wedding
cake design. Natalie has since
won a further four gold awards and
is really looking forward, now that the
book is finished, to having the time to
compete again!

She has written and filmed tutorials
for a number of cake magazines,
including Cake Decoration and
Sugarcraft, Cake International, Cake
Masters, Cakeflix and Cake Decorating
Heaven, having had a number of cover
features over the years.

Back in 2016 she released the Rapid
Rose, the first of a range of products
designed to make the creation of
gorgeous sugar flowers easy and
accessible for everyone.

Live demos and teaching are still
Natalie's favourite thing as nothing
beats the experience of being with
like-minded folk, working together
to create beautiful things...

THANK YOU

I think I could probably write a whole other book just to give thanks to all the people who have believed in me and helped me to get where I am over the years!

To Mel and Leeanne, I give a most heartfelt thanks - it was your faith in me, publishing all those cake tutorials over the years, that gave seed to the idea of writing a book. Had Mel and I not spoken one afternoon back in 2014, I doubt I would be sitting here now with a book in print!

The awesome people at Aitch Creative, that's you Dean and Lynn, have made this book look amazing! Their eye for graphic design has turned this into something that is not only instructional, but also beautiful. It's fair to say that they've done their share of propping me up and encouraging me along on those parts that were particularly tricky to produce, for which I am very grateful.

I would like to thank Sharon Cooper for some beautiful photos and my cousin Andrew - without his patient lessons, acquainting me with my camera, there would be no book!

My friends and family have been an enormous support, putting up with my having disappeared for weeks on end whilst in the midst of a creative flurry. To name but a few I'm particularly grateful to Stephanie & Sam, Susan, Kay, Sophie, Holly, Jo, Andy & Mark, and Jess, I love you guys and you have helped to keep me sane!

And finally I've left the best 'till last.

Verona, my cake bestie, who has been a bottomless source of encouragement and support, reading never ending versions of this book, helping me at shows and providing a sane, calm voice at the end of the phone - I don't think I would have made it without you!

My thanks to my parents, who have listened to endless versions of plans and ideas over the years, offering valuable advice for both life and business. Without my father's patience, advice and business cleverness over the years I wouldn't have made it so far as I have - thank you, Daddy!

My husband, Chris, is my rock. He will hate that I'm putting this into print, but without his love, care and patience, I simply wouldn't have done any of this. Since the beginning he has stood by me and kept me going on the emotional rollercoaster that is being self employed in a creative industry. He is the bestest and I love him. He's the one in the top hat, next time you see him at a show give him a wee hug as none of this would have been possible without him.

www.immaculateconfections.co.uk